FOREWORD

"McClellan is an able general but a very cautious one. His army is in a very demoralized and chaotic condition and will not be prepared for offensive operations -- or he will not think so -- for three or four weeks. By that time I hope to be on the Susquehanna."

Robert E. Lee, Sep 8, 1862

"To the President: I have the whole rebel force in front of me...I have a difficult task to perform but with God's blessing will accomplish it. I think Lee has made a gross mistake and he will be severely punished for it. The army is in motion as rapidly as possible.

Geo. B. McClellan, Sep 13, 1862

After crushing Pope's army at the Second Battle of Bull Run (Manassas), 28-30 August 1862, General Robert E. Lee felt that the time was right to invade the North. Such an operation had been in Lee's mind for some time, and he believed it would improve the Confederacy's chances for recognition by England and France, an extremely important factor in view of the strong Union blockade of Southern ports. The presence of his army in Maryland might shift that border state into the Confederate column, plus the Northern countryside could provide a rich source of supply while giving Northern Virginia farmers a respite from hungry soldiers. Consequently, Lee's Army of Northern Virginia began crossing the Potomac into Maryland near Leesburg on September 5, 1862.

Meanwhile, Major General George B. McClellan, purposely left without orders after his failure to capture Richmond during the peninsula campaign, returned to command the Army of the Potomac. On September 7, he marched north with 84,000 men to oppose Lee's 51,000. By the afternoon of September 15 the armies faced each other across Antietam Creek near the town of Sharpsburg, Maryland. After a day and a half of preparations, McClellan opened the battle at dawn on the 17th when Union General Joseph Hooker's I Corps attacked Stonewall Jackson's battle lines north of the town. More men were killed and wounded on that day than on any other single day of the Civil War. Federal losses were 12,469, Confederate losses were 10,292. Although neither side gained a decisive victory, Lee's failure to carry the war into the North effectively caused England to postpone recognition of the Confederate States. The battle also gave President Lincoln the opportunity to issue the Emancipation Proclamation, which on January 1, 1863, declaring free all slaves in states still in rebellion against the United States. Now the war had a dual purpose: to preserve the Union and free the slaves. Given political effects of the battle, Antietam was arguably the most important battle of the Civil War.

How was so much blood shed on one small battlefield (12 square miles) in one day? And why did Lee choose to fight with his back to the Potomac River? And finally, why did McClellan fail to destroy this underfed, poorly equipped, rag-tag Army of Northern Virginia?

i

These and other questions can only be answered by a visit to the actual terrain over which the battle was fought and a careful analysis of the decisions made by the leaders involved, based on the imformation they had at the time.

Called staff rides, such exercises are not new to the Army. In 1906, Major Eben Swift took twelve officer-students from Fort Leavenworth's General Service and Staff School on the Army's first staff ride to the Chickamauga Battlefield. Since then staff rides have been used to varying degrees in the education of Army officers to narrow the gap between peacetime training and war. That gap is of special concern in today's Army in which few leaders have experienced the stresses of combat. The staff ride, therefore, not only assists participants to understand the realities of war, it teaches warfighting, and in turn enhances unit readiness. It is a training method which commanders can use for the professional development of their subordinates and to enliven the unit's esprit de corps -- constant objectives of all commanders in peacetime.

At some time in their careers most officers have memorized many well-known maxims of the military art, probably without fully understanding or analyzing them. Now, whether you think of yourself as a tactician, operational artist, strategist, or just a soldier as you walk this battlefield, you should search for those operational principles and human characteristics which do not change over time. Place yourself in the minds of the leaders in the battle and analyze the factors involved in their decisions and determine if they could have done better. Only in this way can you fix in your mind the thought processes that must be second nature to you in the crisis of combat.

We are convinced that the staff ride is one of the best ways to do this.

Billy Arthur   Ted Ballard

TABLE OF CONTENTS

Antietam

by Jay Luvaas
(Reproduced with permission of the author)
Maps are included at the end of the text.

"The night after the battle...was a fearful one...The dead and dying lay as thick over [the field] as harvest sheaves. The pitiful cries for water with appeals for help were much more horrible to listen to than the deadliest sounds of battle. Silent were the dead, and motionless. But here and there were raised stiffened arms; heads made a last effort to lift themselves from the ground; prayers were mingled with oaths, the oaths of delirium, men were wriggling over the earth; and midnight hid all distinction between the blue and the gray..."

So wrote an officer on "Stonewall" Jackson's staff. The view from the Union headquarters was equally sobering. "The night brought with it grave responsibilities," reported the commander of the Army of the Potomac. "Whether to renew the attack on the 18th or to defer it...was the question...After a night of anxious deliberation, and in full and careful survey of the situation and condition of our army...I concluded that the success of an attack was not certain...I should have had a narrow view of the condition of the country had I been willing to hazard another battle with less than absolute assurance of success."

All the next day the two armies eyed each other uneasily across the slopes of Sharpsburg ridge. Pleasant and tranquil today, the fields then were so strewn with dead and unattended wounded that the sight seared in General James Longstreet's memory was "too fearful to contemplate." The Confederates, although "worn and exhausted," prepared for a renewal of combat, but MG George B. McClellan lacked the heart to attack. By late afternoon the threat had passed on and Gen Robert E. Lee began issuing orders for the withdrawal. That night, as the glare of the campfire belied their intentions, his men pulled out of their lines, filed to the river ford, and recrossed the Potomac. "Thank God," muttered Lee when at last his proud army stood in comparative safety upon the [West] Virginia bluffs overlooking the river.

The retreat marked the end of the Maryland campaign which had begun with bright hopes just two weeks before. Fresh from earlier success (in June they had turned back one Union thrust against Richmond, and in a recent series of battles around Bull Run had driven another army into the defenses of Washington), Lee's Army of Northern Virginia splashed across the Potomac in early September 1862 and embarked on the Confederacy's first invasion of the North. By the 7th the Confederates had concentrated about Frederick, while the Union army, which McClellan had just reorganized with remarkable speed and efficiency, slowly moved out toward Rockville where it might cover both Washington and Baltimore.

Lee had broader objectives in crossing the Potomac than just "to procure substance" for his troops. "The people of the South have long wished to aid you in throwing off the foreign yoke, to enable you to again enjoy the inalienable rights of freeman, and restore independence and sovereignty to your state," he declared in a proclamation to the people of Maryland on September 8. "In obedience to this wish, our army has come among you..." But Lee found little sympathy in the state. Anticipating that his invasion would cause the Union forces to evacuate Harpers Ferry and Martinsburg, he then planned to shift his line of communications

1

to the west and threaten to carry the war into Pennsylvania. In this way he could maintain his army at the expense of the enemy while drawing the Army of the Potomac away from the Virginia front and its own base of supplies. If Lee's ultimate purpose was to bring his enemy to battle, he did not reveal it in his dispatches to President Jefferson Davis, though he knew that a military victory on Northern soil would do much to win foreign diplomatic recognition for the South.

On September 9, Lee issued Special Order 191 covering the next phase of the campaign. His army would divide before it crossed the Blue Ridge; MG James Longstreet would remain at Boonsboro with two divisions and the baggage trains, MG D. H. Hill's division would constitute a rear guard, while MG Thomas J. ("Stonewall") Jackson with three columns would pinch off the Union garrison at Harpers Ferry. Once in control of that strategic point, Lee's line of communication through the Shenandoah Valley would be secure and he could then march into Pennsylvania.

The bulk of Lee's army moved out from Frederick on September 10 (**see map 1**). MG Lafayette McLaws marched with two divisions by way of Burkittsville into Pleasant Valley and then pushed along the crest of Maryland Heights, which his troops won after a sharp skirmish on the 13th. BG J. G. Walker crossed the Potomac with his division at Point of Rocks during the night of the 10th after a vain attempt to destroy the Monacacy aqueduct of the Chesapeake and Ohio Canal, spent the next day resting in camp, and on the 14th moved into position with his artillery on Loudoun Heights, which dominated most of the Union works protecting Harpers Ferry. Jackson's three divisions forded the Potomac at Williamsport on the 11th, entered Martinsburg the next morning, and completed the investment of Harpers Ferry when they arrived before Bolivar Heights on the 13th.

Lee's plan was based upon the assumption that the Union army would be too disorganized - and its commander too cautious - to exploit this division of his forces, which violated a fundamental principle of strategy. But on September 13, as Jackson's columns converged upon Harpers Ferry, a Union private picked up a lost copy of Lee's order, presenting McClellan with a glittering opportunity "to cut the enemy in two and beat him in detail." Now it was his turn to take the initiative.

On September 14, McClellan's advance divisions fought their way through the gaps at South Mountain, defended at Turner's Gap by D. H. Hill's division with reinforcements from Longstreet's corps, and at Crampton's Gap by three brigades from McLaws' command and two regiments of dismounted cavalry (**see map 2**). This delaying action enabled Lee to concentrate at Sharpsburg and await the arrival of Jackson's force after the capture of Harpers Ferry. He now hoped to reunite his army and fight a successful battle on Maryland soil. The outlook brightened considerably when word arrived on the 15th that Harpers Ferry had surrendered that morning, yielding a prize of more than 11,000 prisoners and significant quantities of guns and military stores. More important, Jackson's divisions would soon be available.

More than Harpers Ferry was lost to the Union when McClellan gave Lee the extra day to prepare for battle. His own army had beaten Jackson in the race to catch up with Lee, so by nightfall of the 15th he had four corps and part of a fifth within easy striking distance of the Confederates. An advance early on the 16th would have caught the Confederates outnumbered by better than three to one, but it never came.

2

Instead of a battle there were only sporadic artillery exchanges throughout the 16th. After "a severe night's march," Jackson arrived during the day with two of his divisions and the one commanded by J. G. Walker. Toward evening the Union I Corps, commanded by "Fighting Joe" Hooker, probed for weak spots on the Confederate left - a sure warning of where the weight of McClellan's attack would fall the next morning. By waiting a day McClellan gave Lee time to reassemble the bulk of his scattered army and bring to the field about 40,000 men to oppose his own 87,000.

Lee's line stretched across the angle formed by the junction of the Potomac and Antietam Creek (**see map 3**). Unable to prevent a Union crossing of the latter to the north, he at least was able to take advantage of the natural defenses of the terrain. The limestone outcroppings and patches of woods offered good cover from the superior weight and numbers of the Union artillery, while the ravines and slight depressions made it possible to rush reinforcements in relative security from one danger spot to another. On a hill two miles north of Sharpsburg and west of the Hagerstown turnpike he posted artillery and some of "Jeb" Stuart's cavalry as support for the Confederate left. The West Woods and the fields east of the turnpike contained two of Jackson's divisions, facing north, with John B. Hood's exhausted division - pulled out of the line after clashing with Hooker the evening before - near the Dunkard Church in support. D. H. Hill's division occupied the center of Lee's line, with his 3,000 men stretching for over a mile. Longstreet's command embraced Hill's position in the sunken road, extended to the bluffs overlooking the Lower Bridge, and curled around to the west to guard the right flank against any attempt to ford the Antietam farther down. Robert Toombs' brigade blocked the passage of the bridge; the rest of D. R. Jones' division held the heights in front of Sharpsburg, while J. G. Walker's division was stationed on the extreme right. Although he had nearly two days in which to prepare his position, Lee erected no breastworks; it was too early in the war apparently, to appreciate the need for artificial cover in the field. He was inferior in artillery, and he lacked reserves except for Hood's division, which was committed to come to the early aid of Jackson. There remained, of course, the three additional divisions on their way from Harpers Ferry, but that morning these hardly counted.

McClellan had intended to attack both Confederate flanks and then, with his reserves, assault Lee's center - a risky plan, since it required a double envelopment (by forces separated by the Antietam) of an enemy well posted and in a better position to send reinforcements wherever needed. And it all miscarried. "The main attack upon the enemy's left" became hardly more than a series of blows by individual divisions as they reached the battlefield, while Burnside's attack against Lee's right was late in materializing. There was no cohesion, no unified command, no definite objective, and at the climax of battle McClellan was unwilling to commit his reserves in the center. Antietam was in fact a soldier's battle, waged by separate units with little direction from above.

The battle began at daybreak with Hooker's assault on the Confederate left. Advancing on a front of two divisions, with a third in reserve, the I Corps drove for the high ground near the Dunkard Church. The leading brigades of each division deployed from columns ten ranks in depth into standard battle formation - skirmishers in front, followed by a continuous line two ranks deep, with a second line some distance to the rear. As the battle developed, these reserve brigades were moved forward to build up the firing line and extend the flanks until

3

the entire corps was engaged. Massed batteries of artillery on a ridge behind Hooker's corps and on the eastern bluffs of the Antietam brought Jackson's line under a deadly crossfire.

In a cornfield, the cornfield, the three of Jackson's brigades tangled with Hooker. Aided by artillery, which raked the field with canister until "every stalk of corn" in the northern part "was cut as closely as could have been with a knife," the I Corps gradually forced the Confederates to yield. "The slain lay in rows , precisely as they had stood in their ranks a few moments before," Hooker reported, adding, "It was never my fortune to witness a more bloody, dismal battlefield." Two of the Confederate brigades lost more than half their number in killed or wounded; the third lost over 30 percent, and only two of the fifteen regimental commanders who saw action escaped injury.

Jackson's other division, in line across the turnpike and west of the cornfield, faced the same terrible fire. Although they stubbornly contested the ground, "sometimes driving the enemy before them and sometimes compelled to fall back before their well-sustained and destructive fire," the men of Jackson's old division were swept back into the West Woods. According to Jackson, "the carnage on both sides was terrific." A Union general later wrote that "the two lines almost tore each other to pieces."

As Hooker's troops fought their way across the fields, they were hit in turn by a violent counterattack by Hood's division, coming up from the Dunkard Church (**see map 4**). "Hood's men always fight well," commented another Confederate general in his official report. That day they fought like devils. In what Hood himself described as "the most terrible clash of arms, by far, that has occurred during the war," his two "little giant brigades" smashed into the divisions of Meade and Doubleday. Jubal Early's brigade, detached to support Stuart's cavalry on the Confederate left, successfully attacked the flank and rear of one of Doubleday's brigades which had formed in line of battle west of the Hagerstown pike. Tired, disorganized, with his reserves engaged, ammunition in short supply, and casualties running high (Rickett's lost one-third of his command and a brigade in another division reported casualties of nearly 40 percent), Hooker's corps withdrew to fight no more as a unit that day.

Once again the cornfield became a storm center as Hood's troops, soon reinforced on the right by three brigades sent over by D. H. Hill, swept the crumbling Union formations back upon their batteries. In the East Woods, Hill's brigades encountered the fresh troops of Mansfield's XII Corps, moving up to support Hooker. Williams' division (Mansfield was mortally wounded early in the action and Williams assumed command of the corps) deployed on the right; "after a severe struggle of an hour and a half" Williams' brigades drove the Confederates back into the West Woods (**see map 5**). Meanwhile Greene's division, on the left of this new Union battleline, engaged the Confederates among the thick trees and rock ledges of the East Woods. "After a short but severe contest" Greene's veteran division, weakened by the detachment of one brigade to bolster the extreme right flank of the Union line, pushed past Hill's brigades on their extreme left and forged ahead to the field beyond the burning Mumma House. Here it paused to regroup and replenish ammunition.

It was now 9 o'clock, and more Union troops were massing behind the East Woods for still another assault (**see map 6**). This was Sedgwick's division of Edwin V. Sumner's II Corps, which had forded the Antietam that morning and was now advancing toward the West Woods and three brigade lines 60 to 70 paces apart. On they came, nearly 6,000 of them, through the East Woods - by this time littered with the human debris of both armies - across the cornfield, where they came under heavy artillery fire, and into the West Woods. Only Early's brigade and the remnants of one of Jackson's divisions were on hand to hold the line until reinforcements could be rushed from another part of the field. Gliding beneath the crest of the hill in front of Sedgwick, Early worked his men around to the left front corner of the Union column. Here he was soon joined by McLaws' division, which had arrived from Harpers Ferry a short time before, and Walker's division, which had been shifted over from its original position on the Confederate right. This counterthrust by forces at least the equal of Sedgwick and probably larger, and aimed at the most vulnerable part of the column, the flanks, saved the day for Lee. Sedgwick's third line was the first to give way. Then in confusion the second line opened fire and killed many of those in the front ranks, and because their formation was too compact, the Union troops could not deploy in the direction of the Confederate attack. "The fire came upon them from front and flank and presently from the rear." Within minutes the ground was strewn with 2,200 casualties and Sedgwick's entire division was in retreat.

Again, the Confederates swarmed northward in pursuit. Williams' division had already retired to the vicinity of the East Woods, and Sedgwick's troops took refuge behind "a long line of strong post and rail fences." Unable to overcome this obstacle and even to stand long under an incessant storm of shot and shell, grape and canister," McLaws and Walker were forced to fall back and take shelter in the West Woods, where they continued to come under fire of Union artillery. The Confederate counterattack also beat against Greene's division and provoked it into further action. After repulsing two assaults this small division surged forward to the West Woods near the Dunkard Church, where it staunchly held its ground for nearly two hours. About noon the division was withdrawn to the main line, and the battle on Lee's left was virtually over. When Sumner's remaining divisions came up, the battle entered a new - and for McClellan and unexpected - phase. French, forming his division into three brigade lines, did not follow Sedgwick into the West Woods but instead veered south, leaving Greene's division at the Dunkard Church to plug the gap between the two divisions. This line of advance brought him to the Roulette farm, where he encountered elements of D. H. Hill's division. French's division drove forward to a hill north of the sunken road, where Hill's brigades under Rodes and G. B. Anderson were preparing to make a stand. Although commanded by high ground to the north and east, this narrow lane with bordering rail fences served as a natural trench. R. H. Anderson's division, which had arrived from Harpers Ferry that morning, moved into the field to the south in support (**see map** 7). As French's division surged forward, it reached a crest overlooking the sunken road. A Confederate brigadier described what happened next: "While the men were busy improving their position by piling rails along their front, the enemy deployed in our front in three beautiful lines, all vastly outstretching ours, and commenced to advance...to the crest of the hill...and for five minutes bravely stood a telling fire at 80 yards, which my whole brigade delivered. They then fell back a short distance, rallied, were driven back again and again, and finally lay down just back of the crest, keeping up a steady fire..." One Union colonel reported that he held his position only "at a fearful sacrifice. The men were supplied with 60 rounds of ammunition, and exhausted their supply, and took the cartridges from the dead and wounded, and kept up the fire against the enemy." Hill's men tried on several occasions to outflank French, but the arrival of Israel B. Richardson's division of the II Corps decided the outcome. Swinging into line on the left of French, Richardson's division was able to enfilade the Confederate line and convert the sunken road into a "Bloody Lane." The momentum of this charge carried the Union troops all the way into the Piper orchard, near the Hagerstown Pike, and for a few desperate moments Longstreet's center was held by remnants of several disorganized brigades, one a North Carolina regiment without ammunition, and four fieldpieces served in part by Longstreet's staff (**see map 8**). But Richardson received a mortal wound, and his men were unable to sustain their offensive. When they withdrew a short distance to higher ground shortly after noon, the battle in the center died down.

It flared up next on the Confederate right, where McClellan had been prodding Ambrose Burnside for several hours (since 10 a.m., he said in his initial report; later he claimed that he sent his first order to Burnside at 8 o'clock) to storm the bridge and the heights beyond. The first attempt by Crook's brigade went astray; a second column, charging with fixed bayonets, likewise withered before the galling fire that Toombs' infantry and the flanking batteries concentrated upon the bridge. Finally, at 1 p.m. two regiments, the 51st New York and the 51st Pennsylvania , dashed across the bridge and gained a foothold on the western bank, while Rodman's division outflanked the Confederate position by fording the creek farther down (**see map 9**). But it took three vital hours for Burnside's battleline to advance up the slopes from the bridgehead. By later afternoon the IX Corps had almost pushed into the village of Sharpsburg (**see map 10**). Once again Lee's line was stretched to the breaking point when fresh reinforcements, this time the celebrated light division under A. P. Hill, arrived to hit Burnside's left flank. Covering the seventeen miles from Harpers Ferry in seven hours, Hill's division forced Burnside to retreat to the heights above the bridge. The battle of Antietam was over.

Thus the campaign that had taken such a dramatic turn four days earlier with the chance discovery of a lost order culminated in a battle of many lost opportunities for the Union. Had McClellan attacked on the 16th; had the attack of the I, II and XII Corps been better coordinated; had French and Richardson but realized how close they were to snapping the Confederate line and had the fresh corps of Franklin (which was only lightly engaged) and Porter been thrown into the battle at this point; had Burnside been aggressive enough on the early hours to prevent Lee from stripping his right to reinforce Jackson and Hood - had any of these opportunities been grasped, the results must have been a great victory. McClellan might have seized the hill behind the West Wood that dominated the Confederate left and thrown the weight of his attack against the exposed flank. He should have made still better use of massed artillery and thrown division upon division against Lee's line until it broke. But McClellan lacked such an instinct to grab for the jugular. Afraid to commit his reserves, he kept his cavalry in the center, where they could serve no useful purpose; he failed to see that his subordinate commanders carried out his overall design. He could have renewed the assault the next day with odds still more in his favor. Instead he rested his troops and awaited reinforcements (some of which had arrived by 7 a.m.), while Lee remained in position throughout the 18th, then slipped across the Potomac that night.

If Antietam was fought badly by McClellan, it was a battle that Lee should never have fought at all. His army was depleted from recent battles and strenuous marches, and the numbers he faced were too formidable to offer any real prospect of success. If he had defeated McClellan on the west side of the Antietam, what could he have done next? A frontal assault against the overpowering artillery placed on the hills across the Antietam would have been out of the question, and the terrain did not lend itself to any large scale maneuver on the flanks. Even "Stonewall" Jackson was forced to abandon plans for a flank attack against the Union right. Admirers of Lee have alleged that there were valid political and psychological reasons why he chose to offer battle in Maryland, that he "had read McClellan's innermost soul and knew he was not to be feared." Perhaps so. The fact remains that Lee needlessly courted military disaster under tactical conditions that made the chances for victory remote. Success, if won, could not have been exploited because of the nature of the terrain and the overwhelming strength of the Union army. The most the Lee could reasonably have hoped for was a standoff. That this ultimately happened was primarily the result of the high degree of coordination and cooperation among the Confederate troops and the division commanders, as opposed to the lack of any supreme will or direction on the part of the Union generals. The rosy results, strategic and diplomatic, that might have followed a Confederate victory along the Antietam in no way improved Lee's field position, while the victory that McClellan might well have won could easily have brought the war to a more speedy end.

A tactical draw, this convulsive struggle represented a strategic defeat for the South, for Lee had to postpone his invasion of Pennsylvania. Yet the benefits to the North were essentially political. The battle made possible Lincoln's Emancipation Proclamation, which changed both the objectives and the character of the war and greatly reduced the chances of either foreign intervention or recognition of the Confederacy.

Antietam might have ended the war; instead it only prolonged it. The official reports, the eloquent testimony of survivors, and the men left behind in field hospitals or in shallow graves - 12,410 Union and 10,700 Confederate - all bear witness to the fact that more Americans fell here than any other single day in the Civil War, and probably in any single day of our entire military history.

THE PRY HOUSE, GENERAL McCLELLAN'S HEADQUARTERS AT THE BATTLE OF ANTIETAM. FROM A PHOTOGRAPH TAKEN IN 1886.

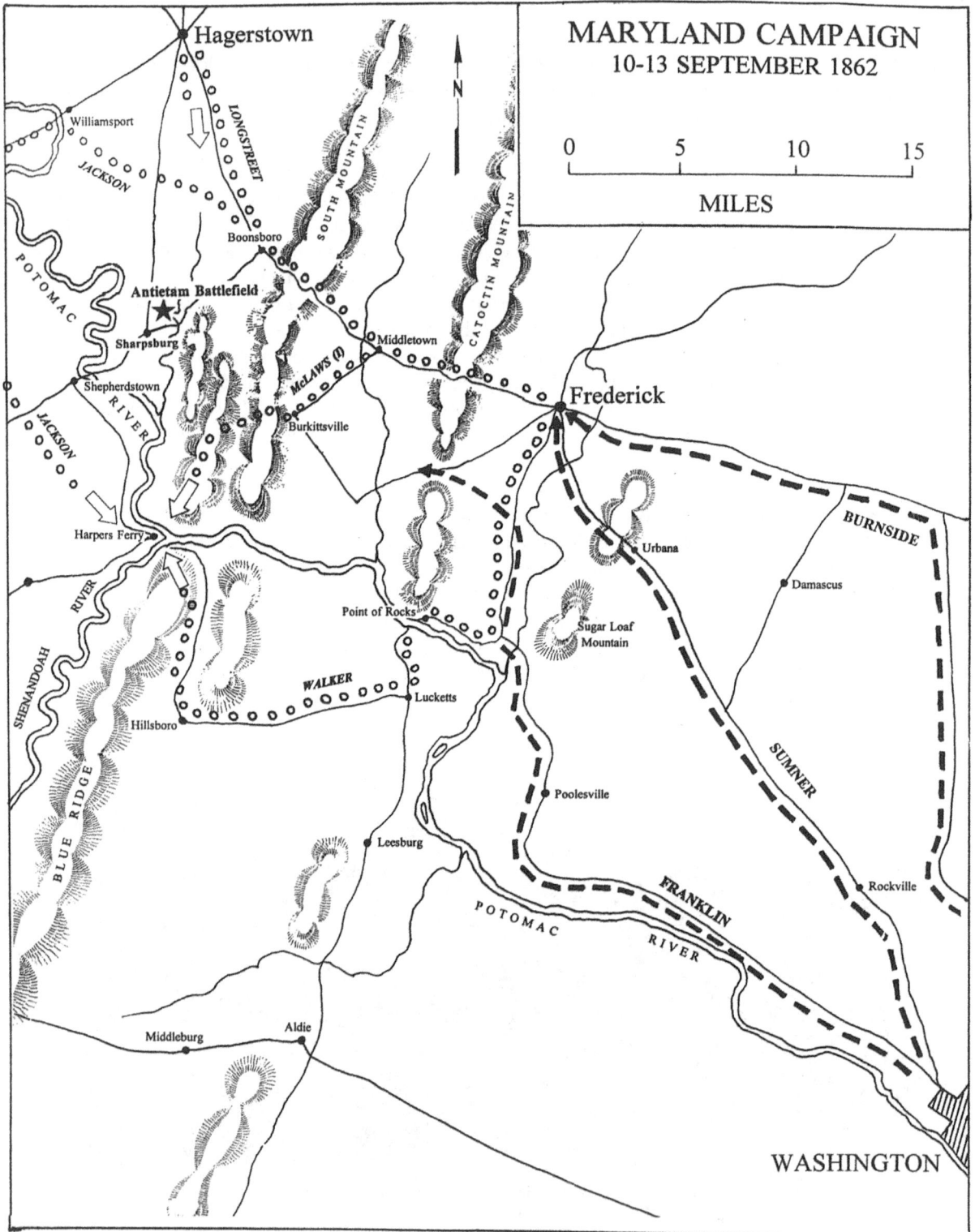

MARYLAND CAMPAIGN
10-13 SEPTEMBER 1862

0   5   10   15
MILES

Hagerstown

Williamsport

JACKSON

LONGSTREET

SOUTH MOUNTAIN

Boonsboro

POTOMAC

Antietam Battlefield

Sharpsburg

Shepherdstown

RIVER

JACKSON

McLAWS (I)

Burkittsville

CATOCTIN MOUNTAIN

Middletown

Frederick

BURNSIDE

Harpers Ferry

SHENANDOAH

RIVER

Hillsboro

BLUE RIDGE

WALKER

Point of Rocks

Lucketts

Urbana

Damascus

Sugar Loaf Mountain

SUMNER

Poolesville

Rockville

Leesville

Leesburg

POTOMAC

FRANKLIN

RIVER

Middleburg

Aldie

WASHINGTON

8

Map 1

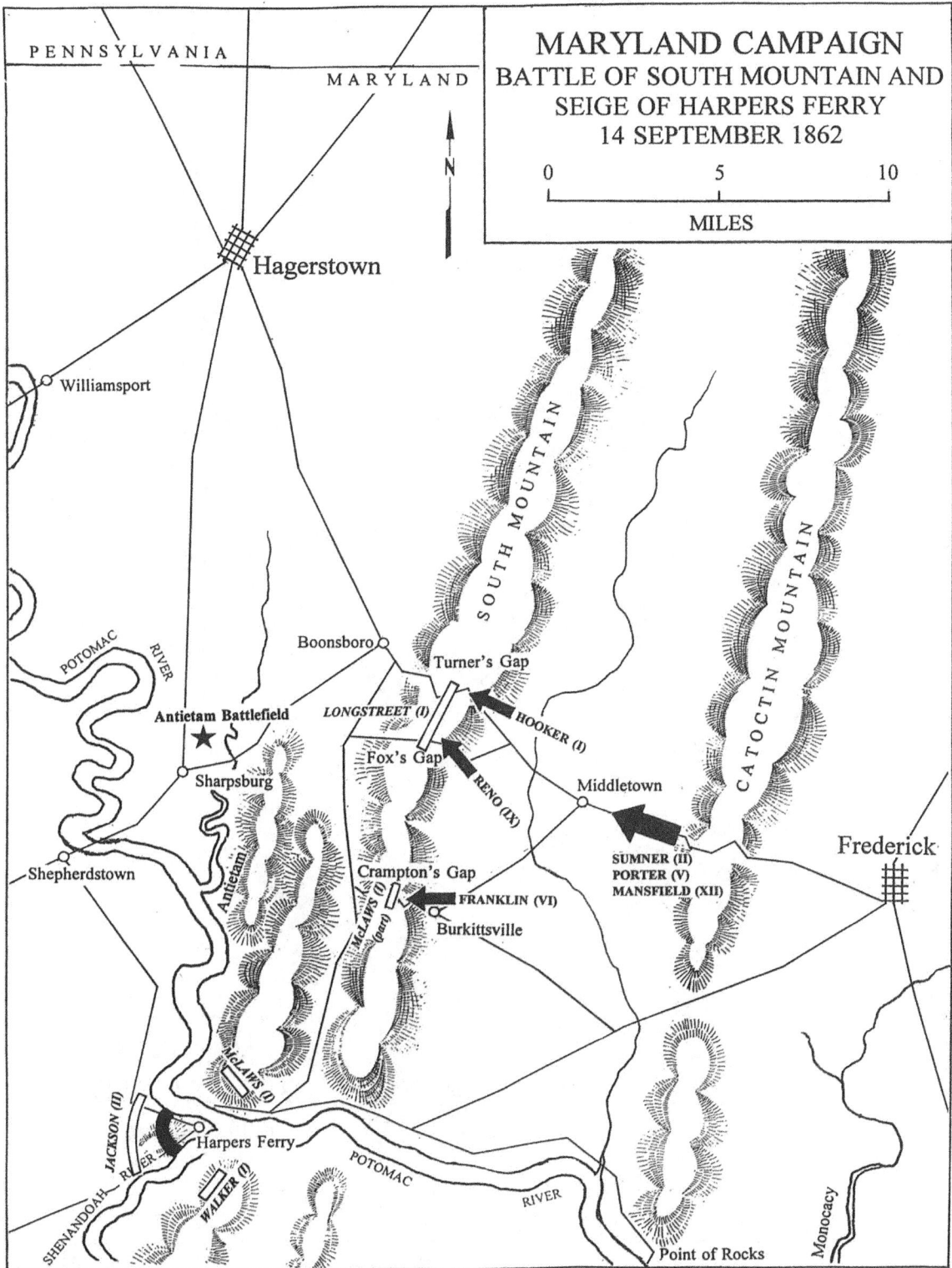

MARYLAND CAMPAIGN
BATTLE OF SOUTH MOUNTAIN AND SEIGE OF HARPERS FERRY
14 SEPTEMBER 1862

```
0                    5                    10
|---------------------|---------------------|
              MILES
```

PENNSYLVANIA

MARYLAND

N

Hagerstown

Williamsport

POTOMAC RIVER

Boonsboro

Turner's Gap

SOUTH MOUNTAIN

CATOCTIN MOUNTAIN

LONGSTREET (I)

HOOKER (I)

Antietam Battlefield

Fox's Gap

RENO (IX)

Middletown

Sharpsburg

Frederick

SUMNER (II)
PORTER (V)
MANSFIELD (XII)

Crampton's Gap

FRANKLIN (VI)

Shepherdstown

McLAWS (I)

McLAWS (part)

Burkittsville

Antietam

JACKSON (II)

Harpers Ferry

SHENANDOAH RIVER

POTOMAC

WALKER (I)

RIVER

Point of Rocks

Monocacy

9

Map 2

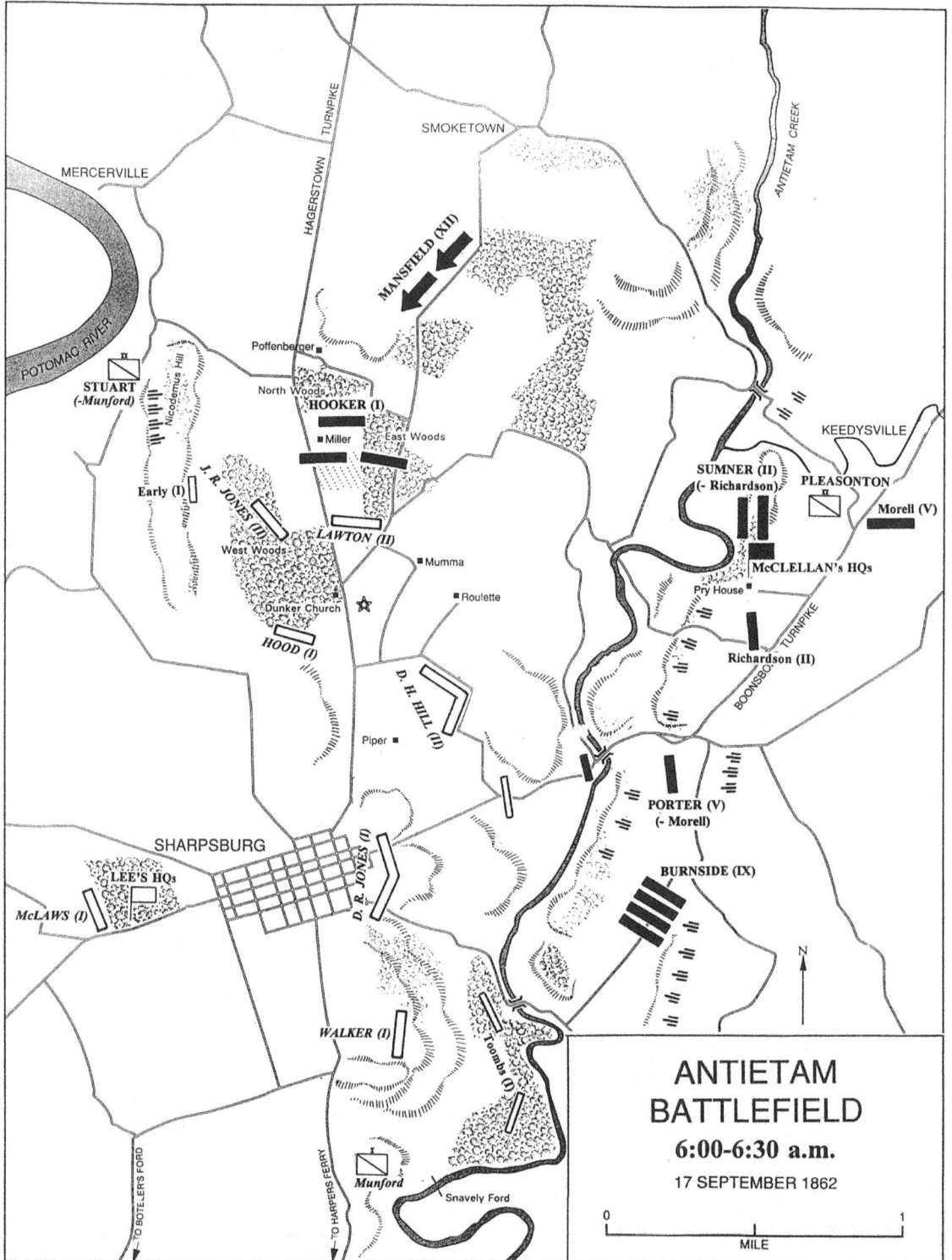

MERCERVILLE

POTOMAC RIVER

HAGERSTOWN TURNPIKE

SMOKETOWN

ANTIETAM CREEK

MANSFIELD (XII)

STUART
(-Munford)

Poffenberger

North Woods

HOOKER (I)

Miller

East Woods

KEEDYSVILLE

Nicodemus Hill

SUMNER (II)
(- Richardson)

PLEASONTON

Morell (V)

Early (I)

J. R. JONES (II)

LAWTON (II)

West Woods

Mumma

McCLELLAN's HQs

Dunker Church

Roulette

Pry House

HOOD (I)

D. H. HILL (II)

Richardson (II)

BOONSBORO TURNPIKE

Piper

PORTER (V)
(- Morell)

SHARPSBURG

LEE'S HQs

D. R. JONES (I)

BURNSIDE (IX)

McLAWS (I)

N

WALKER (I)

Toombs (I)

**ANTIETAM
BATTLEFIELD**

6:00-6:30 a.m.

17 SEPTEMBER 1862

TO BOTELER'S FORD

TO HARPERS FERRY

Munford

Snavely Ford

0   1

MILE

☆ VISITOR CENTER

Map 3

10

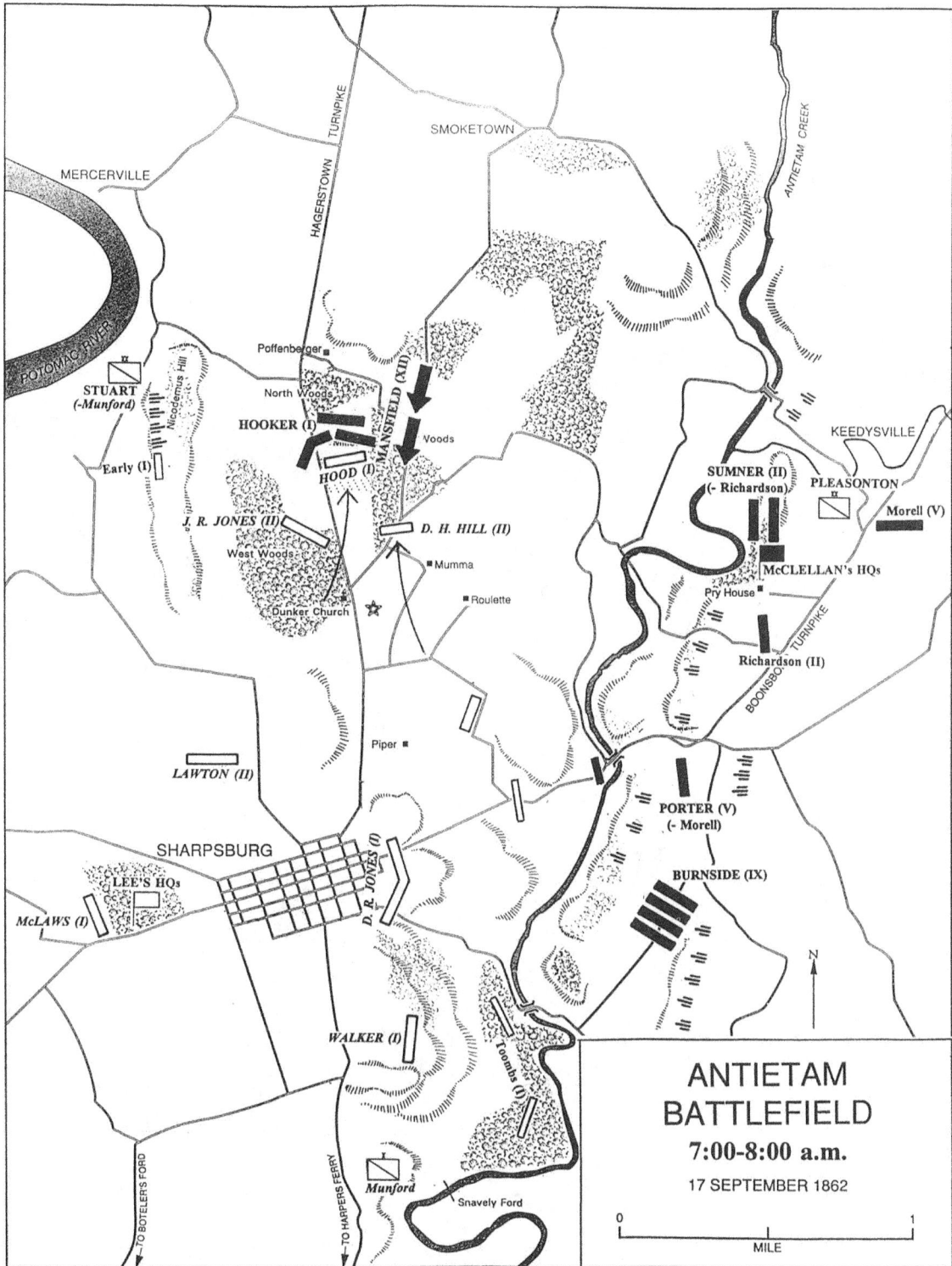

MERCERVILLE

POTOMAC RIVER

SMOKETOWN

HAGERSTOWN TURNPIKE

ANTIETAM CREEK

STUART
(-Munford)

Nicodemus Hill

Poffenberger

North Woods

MANSFIELD (XII)

Voods

KEEDYSVILLE

Early (I)

HOOKER (I)

J. R. JONES (II)

HOOD (I)

West Woods

D. H. HILL (II)

SUMNER (II)
(- Richardson)

PLEASONTON

Morell (V)

Mumma

McCLELLAN's HQs

Dunker Church

Roulette

Pry House

Richardson (II)

BOONSBORO TURNPIKE

Piper

LAWTON (II)

PORTER (V)
(- Morell)

SHARPSBURG

BURNSIDE (IX)

D. R. JONES (I)

LEE'S HQs

McLAWS (I)

N

WALKER (I)

Toombs (I)

**ANTIETAM
BATTLEFIELD**

7:00-8:00 a.m.

17 SEPTEMBER 1862

TO BOTELERS FORD

TO HARPERS FERRY

Munford

Snavely Ford

0   1

MILE

☆ VISITOR CENTER

Map 4

11

MERCERVILLE

POTOMAC RIVER

SMOKETOWN

HAGERSTOWN TURNPIKE

ANTIETAM CREEK

STUART
(-Munford)

Poffenberger

North Woods

HOOKER (I)

SUMNER (II)
(- Richardson)

KEEDYSVILLE

Miller

East Woods

PLEASONTON

Early (I)

Williams (XII)

Morell (V)

Greene (XII)

McCLELLAN's HQs

West Woods

D. H. HILL (II)

Pry House

J. R. JONES (II)

HOOD (I)

Mumma

Dunker Church

Roulette

Richardson (II)

BOONSBORO TURNPIKE

Piper

McLAWS (I)

LAWTON (II)

PORTER (V)
(- Morell)

SHARPSBURG

BURNSIDE (IX)

LEE's HQs

D. R. JONES (I)

WALKER (I)

N

TO SOTELERS FORD

TO HARPERS FERRY

Toombs (I)

Munford

Snavely Ford

ANTIETAM
BATTLEFIELD

8:00-9:00 a.m.
17 SEPTEMBER 1862

0   1
MILE

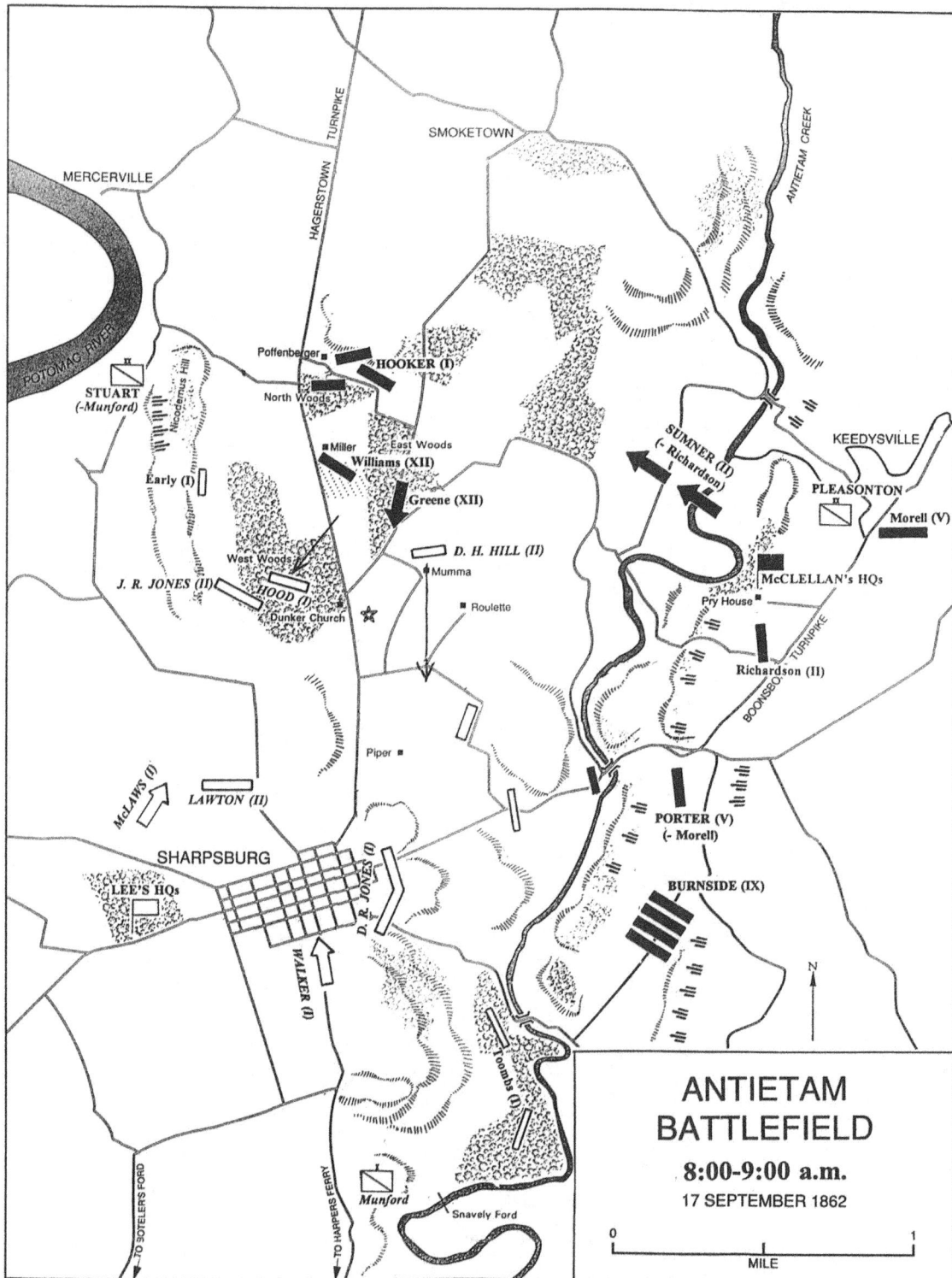

⭐ VISITOR CENTER

Map 5

12

MERCERVILLE

POTOMAC RIVER

SMOKETOWN

HAGERSTOWN TURNPIKE

ANTIETAM CREEK

Poffenbe

HOOKER (I)

North Wo

STUART
(-Munford)

KEEDYSVILLE

Nicodemus Hill

Miller

Williams (XII)

at Woods

Richardson (II)

PLEASONTON

J. R. JONES (II)

Sedgwick (II)

McCLELLAN's HQs

West Woods

Greene (XII)

Mumma

Pry House

Early (I)

McLaws (I)

ch

Roulette

French (II)

WALKER (I)

Jones

HOOD (I)

D. H. HILL (II)

Piper

PORTER (V)

BOONSBORO TURNPIKE

LAWTON (II)

SHARPSBURG

BURNSIDE (IX)

D. R. JONES (I)

LEE'S HQs

N

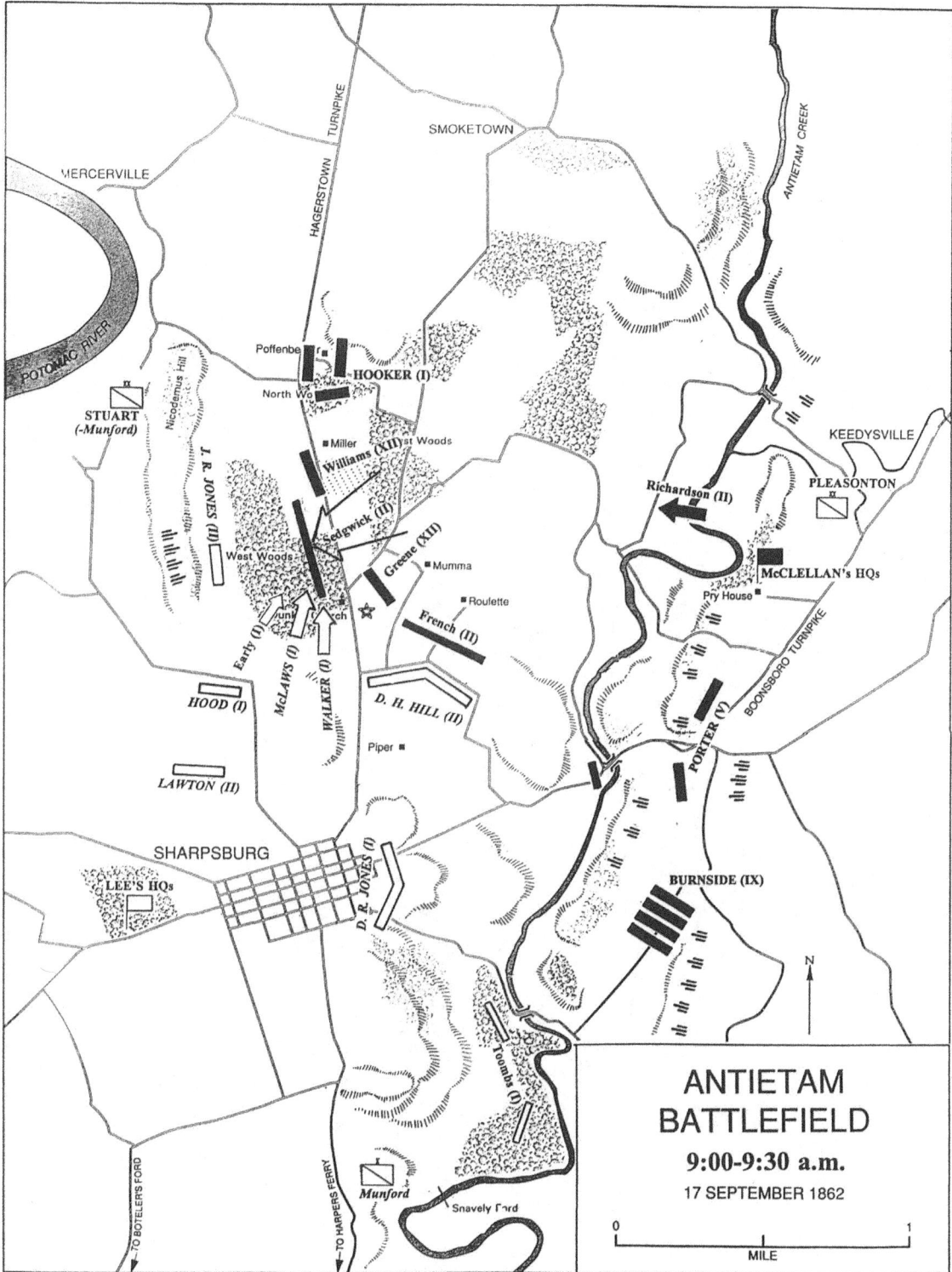

ANTIETAM
BATTLEFIELD

Toombs (I)

9:00-9:30 a.m.

17 SEPTEMBER 1862

TO BOTELER'S FORD

TO HARPERS FERRY

Munford

Snavely Ford

0   1

MILE

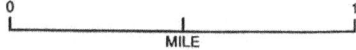

★ VISITOR CENTER

Map 6

13

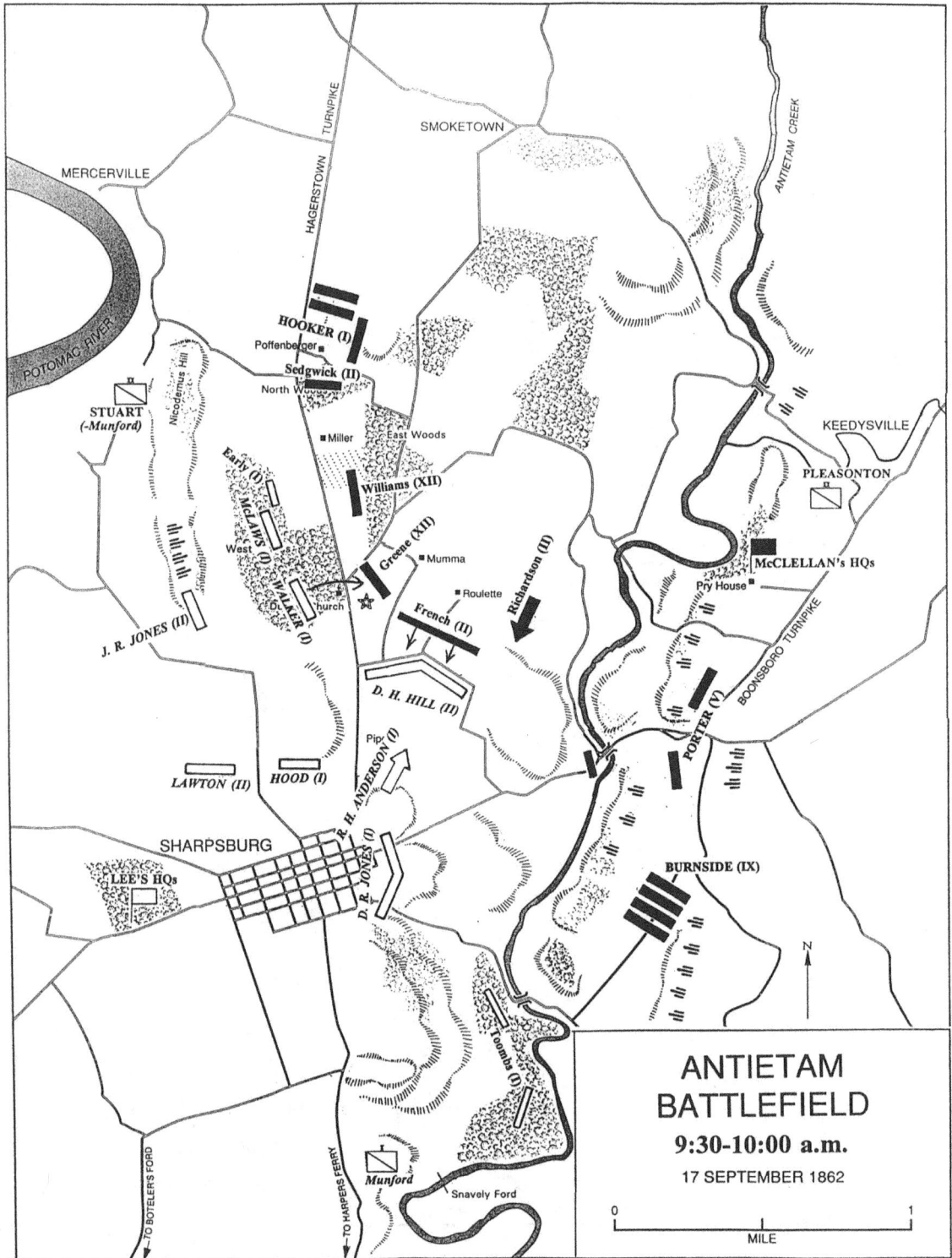

MERCERVILLE

SMOKETOWN

POTOMAC RIVER

HAGERSTOWN TURNPIKE

ANTIETAM CREEK

STUART
(-Munford)

Nicodemus Hill

HOOKER (I)

Poffenberger

Sedgwick (II)

North Woods

Miller

East Woods

KEEDYSVILLE

Early (I)

McLaws (I)

Williams (XII)

PLEASONTON

West

WALKER (I)

Greene (XII)

Mumma

McCLELLAN's HQs

Pry House

Church

Richardson (II)

Roulette

J. R. JONES (II)

French (II)

PORTER (V)

BOONSBORO TURNPIKE

D. H. HILL (II)

LAWTON (II)

HOOD (I)

Pipe (I)

R. H. ANDERSON (I)

SHARPSBURG

BURNSIDE (IX)

LEE'S HQs

D. R. JONES (I)

N

Toombs (I)

ANTIETAM
BATTLEFIELD

9:30-10:00 a.m.

17 SEPTEMBER 1862

TO BOTELERS FORD

TO HARPERS FERRY

Munford

Snavely Ford

0   MILE   1

☆ VISITOR CENTER

Map 7

14

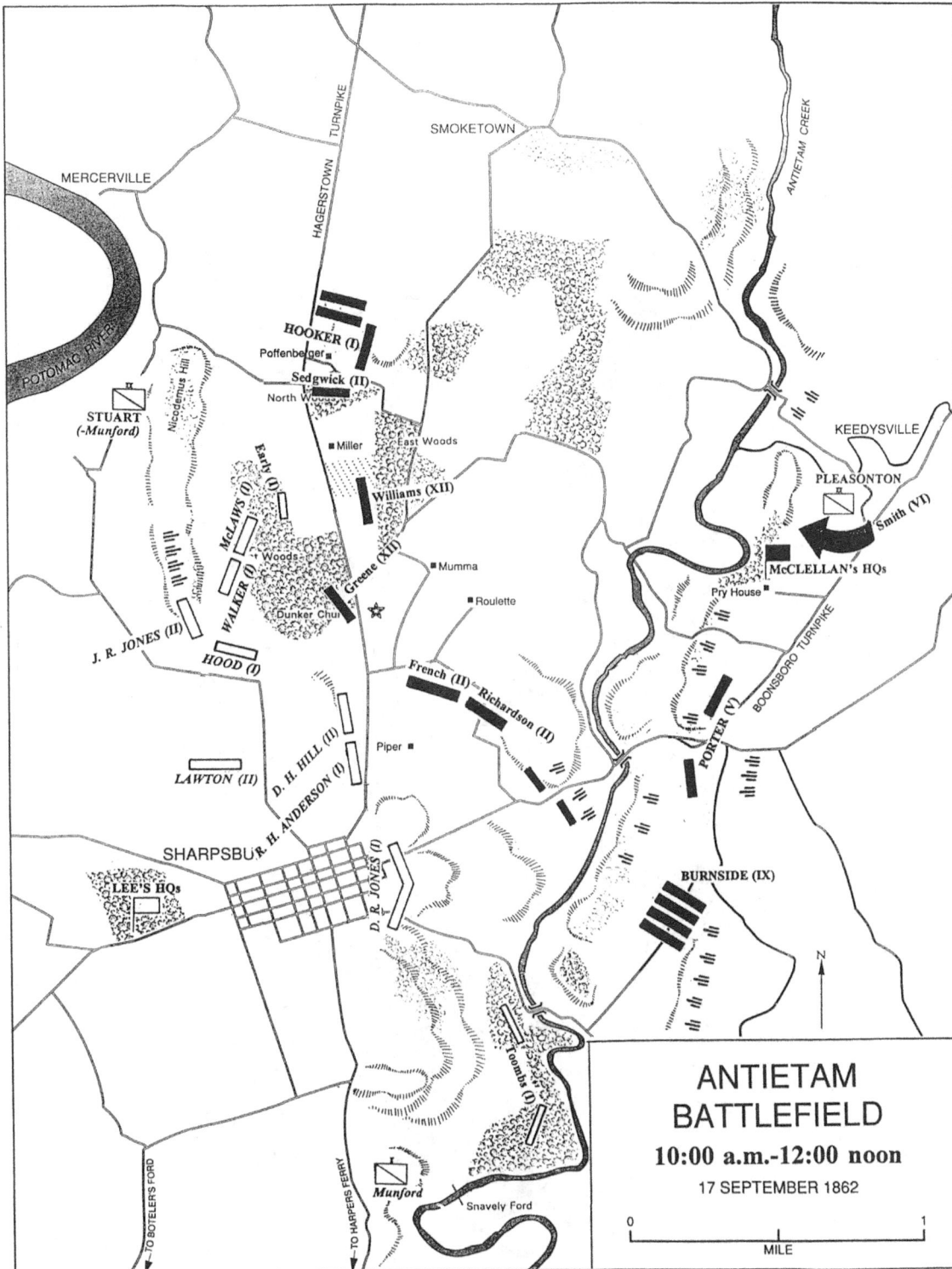

MERCERVILLE

POTOMAC RIVER

HAGERSTOWN TURNPIKE

SMOKETOWN

ANTIETAM CREEK

STUART
(-Munford)

Nicodemus Hill

HOOKER (I)

Poffenberger

Sedgwick (II)

North Woods

KEEDYSVILLE

Early (I)

Miller

East Woods

McLaws (I)

Williams (XII)

PLEASONTON

Smith (VI)

WALKER (I)

Woods

Greene (XII)

Mumma

McCLELLAN's HQs

J. R. JONES (II)

Dunker Church

Roulette

Pry House

HOOD (I)

French (II)

Richardson (II)

PORTER (V)

BOONSBORO TURNPIKE

LAWTON (II)

D. H. HILL (II)

R. H. ANDERSON (I)

Piper

SHARPSBURG

LEE'S HQs

D. R. JONES (I)

BURNSIDE (IX)

N

Toombs (I)

ANTIETAM
BATTLEFIELD
10:00 a.m.–12:00 noon
17 SEPTEMBER 1862

Munford

Snavely Ford

0   1
MILE

TO BOTELERS FORD

TO HARPERS FERRY

☆ VISITOR CENTER

Map 8

15

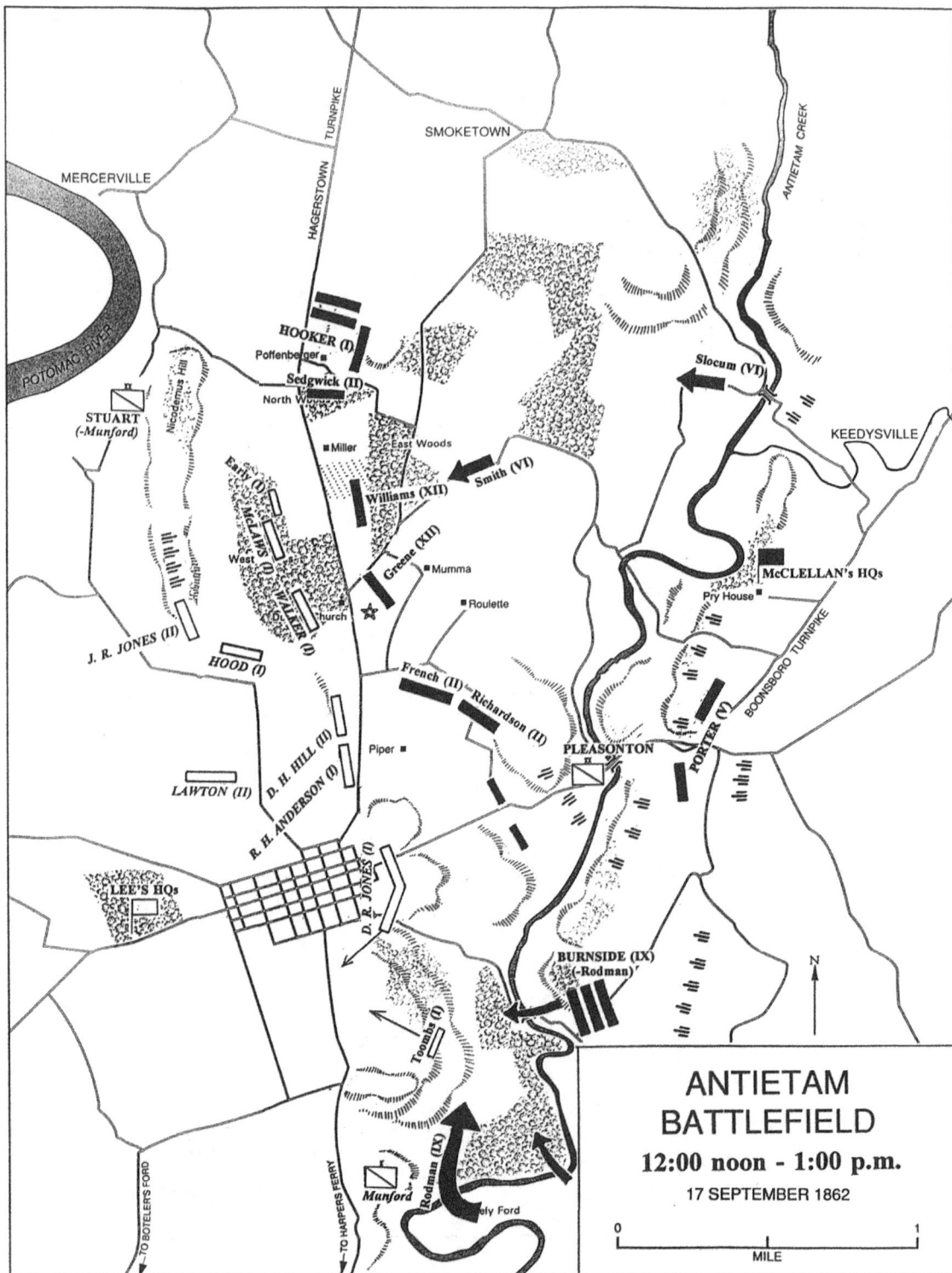

MERCERVILLE

SMOKETOWN

POTOMAC RIVER

ANTIETAM CREEK

HAGERSTOWN TURNPIKE

HOOKER (I)

Poffenberger

Sedgwick (II)

North Woods

Slocum (VI)

KEEDYSVILLE

STUART
(-Munford)

Nicodemus Hill

Miller

East Woods

Early (I)

McLAWS (I)

West Woods

WALKER (I)

Williams (XII)

Smith (VI)

McCLELLAN's HQs

Pry House

Greene (XII)

Mumma

Church

Roulette

J. R. JONES (II)

HOOD (I)

BOONSBORO TURNPIKE

French (II)

Richardson (II)

PORTER (V)

Piper

PLEASONTON

LAWTON (II)

D. H. HILL (II)

D. H. HILL (II)

R. H. ANDERSON (I)

LEE's HQs

D. R. JONES (I)

N

BURNSIDE (IX)
(-Rodman)

Toombs (I)

ANTIETAM
BATTLEFIELD

12:00 noon - 1:00 p.m.

17 SEPTEMBER 1862

TO BOTELER'S FORD

TO HARPERS FERRY

Munford

Rodman (IX)

Ely Ford

0   MILE   1

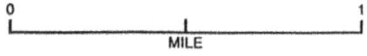

★ VISITOR CENTER

Map 9

16

MERCERVILLE

POTOMAC RIVER

SMOKETOWN

ANTIETAM CREEK

HAGERSTOWN TURNPIKE

HOOKER (I)

Poffenberger

Nicodemus Hill

STUART
(-Munford)

Sedgwick (II)

North Woods

Williams (XII)

Miller

Greene (XII)

KEEDYSVILLE

Early (I)

Slocum (VI)

McLAWS (I)

West Woods

Smith (VI)

WALKER (I)

Roulette

McCLELLAN's HQs

Pry House

Dunker Church

J. R. JONES (II)

HOOD (I)

French (II)

R. H. ANDERSON (I)

Richardson (II)

BOONSBORO TURNPIKE

Piper

LAWTON (II)

PLEASONTON

D. H. HILL (II)

PORTER (V)

SHARPSBURG

LEE'S HQs

Wilcox (IX)

D. R. JONES (I)

Rodman (IX)

Cox (IX)

Sturgis (IX)

A. P. HILL (II)

N

TO BOTELERS FORD

TO HARPERS FERRY

Munford

Snavely Ford

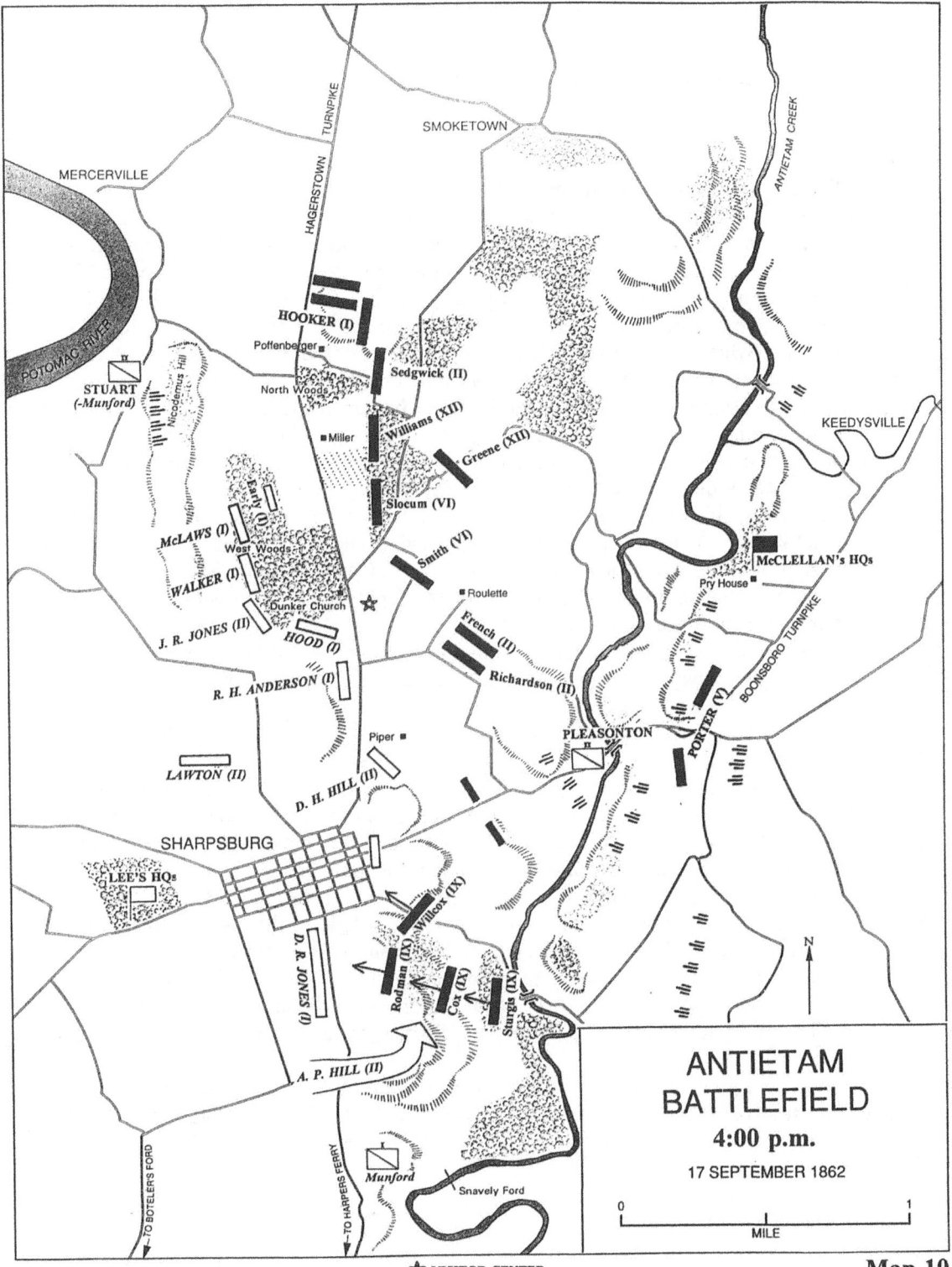

ANTIETAM
BATTLEFIELD
4:00 p.m.
17 SEPTEMBER 1862

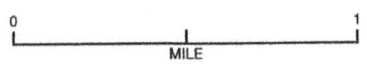

0   1
MILE

★ VISITOR CENTER

Map 10

17

ROBERT E. LEE'S THEATER-LEVEL SITUATION REPORT

Lee to Jefferson Davis, 3 Sep 1862:

"The present seems to be the most propitious time since the commencement of the war for the Confederate Army to enter Maryland. The two grand armies of the United States that have been operating in Virginia, though now united, are much weakened and demoralized. Their new levies, of which I understand sixty thousand men have already been posted in Washington, are not yet organized, and will take some time to prepare for the field. If it is ever desired to give material aid to Maryland and afford her an opportunity of throwing off the oppression to which she now is subject, this would seem the most favorable. After the enemy had disappeared from the vicinity of Fairfax Court House and taken the road to Alexandria and Washington, I did not think it would be advantageous to follow him further... I therefore determined while threatening the approaches to Washington, to draw the troops into Loudoun, where the forage and some provisions can be obtained, menace their possession of the Shenandoah Valley, and if found practicable, to cross into Maryland.

The purpose, if discovered, would have the effect of carrying the enemy north of the Potomac, and if prevented, will not result in much evil. The army is not properly equipped for an invasion of an enemy's territory. It lacks much of the material of war, is feeble in transportation, the animals much reduced, and the men poorly provided with clothes, and in thousands of instances are destitute of shoes.

Still we cannot afford to be idle, and though weaker than our opponents in men and military equipments, must endeavor to harass, if we cannot destroy them..."

Lee to Jefferson Davis, 12 Sep 1862:

"Before crossing the Potomac I considered the advantages of entering Maryland east or west of the Blue Ridge. In either case it was my intention to march upon this town [Hagerstown]. By crossing east of the Blue Ridge, both Washington and Baltimore would be threatened, which I believed would insure withdrawal of the mass of the enemy's troops north of the Potomac. I think this has been accomplished. I had also supposed that as soon as it was known that the army had reached Fredericktown [Frederick], the enemy's forces in the Valley of Virginia, which had retired to Harpers Ferry and Martinsburg, would retreat altogether from the state. In this I was disappointed, and you will perceive from the accompanying order [Special Order, 191] of the 9th instant that Genls Jackson and McLaws have been detached with a view of capturing their forces at each place, should they not have retired.

A thousand pairs of shoes and some clothing were obtained in Fredericktown, two hundred and fifty pairs in Williamsport, and about four hundred pairs in this city. They will not be sufficient to cover the bare feet of the army."

"LEE'S LOST DISPATCH"

SPECIAL ORDERS   HEADQUARTERS ARMY OF NORTHERN VIRGINIA
NO. 191   SEPTEMBER 9, 1862

1. The citizens of Fredericktown being unwilling while overrun by members of this army, to open their stores, in order to give them confidence, and to secure to officers and men purchasing supplies for benefit of this command, all officers and men of this army are strictly prohibited from visiting Fredericktown except on business, in which cases they wear bear evidence of this in writing from division commanders. The provost-marshal in Fredericktown will see that his guard rigidly enforces this order.

2. Major Tyler will proceed to Leesburg, Va., and arrange for transportation of the sick and those unable to walk to Winchester, securing the transportation of the country for this purpose. The route between this and Culpeper Court-House east of the mountains being unsafe, will no longer be travelled. Those on the way to this army already across the river will move up promptly; all others will proceed to Winchester collectively, or under command of officers, at which point, being the general depot of this army, its movements will be known and instructions given by commanding officer regulating further movements.

3. The army will resume its march tomorrow, taking the Hagerstown road. General Jackson's command will form the advance, and, after passing Sharpsburg, cross the Potomac at the most convenient point, and by Friday morning take possession of the Baltimore and Ohio Railroad, capture such of them as may be at Martinsburg, and intercept such as may attempt to escape from Harpers Ferry.

4. General Longstreet's command will pursue the same road as far as Boonsborough, where it will halt, with reserve, supply, and baggage trains of the army.

5. General McLaws, with his own division and that of General R. H. Anderson, will follow General Longstreet. On reaching Middletown will take the route to Harpers Ferry, and by Friday morning possess himself of the Maryland Heights and endeavor to capture the enemy at Harpers Ferry and vicinity.

6. General Walker, with his division, after accomplishing the object in which he is now engaged, will cross the Potomac at Cheek's Ford, ascend its right bank to Lovettsville, take possession of Loudoun Heights, if practicable, by Friday morning, Key's Ford on his left, and the road between the end of the mountain and the Potomac on his right. He will, as far as practicable, cooperate with General McLaws and Jackson, and intercept retreat of the enemy.

7. General D. H. Hill's division will form the rear guard of the army, pursuing the road taken by the main body. The reserve artillery, ordnance, and supply trains, etc., will precede General Hill.

8. General Stuart will detach a squadron of cavalry to accompany the commands of Generals Longstreet, Jackson, and McLaws, and, with the main body of the cavalry, will cover the route of the army, bringing up all stragglers that may have been left behind.

9. The commands of Generals Jackson, McLaws, and Walker, after accomplishing the objects for which they have been detached, will join the main body of the army at Boonsborough or Hagerstown.

10. Each regiment on the march will habitually carry its axes in the regimental ordnance wagons, for use of the men at their encampments, top procure wood, etc.

By Command of General R. E. Lee
R.H. Chilton, Assistant Adjutant-General

GEORGE B. McCLELLAN'S THEATER-LEVEL SITUATION REPORT

McClellan to MG Henry Halleck, General in Chief, 11 September 1862:

"At the time this army moved from Washington, it was not known what the intentions of the Rebels were in placing their forces on this side of the Potomac. It might have been a feint to draw away our troops from Washington, for the purpose of throwing their main army into the city as soon as we were out of the way, or it might have been supposed to be precisely what they are now doing. In view of this uncertain condition of things, I left what I conceived to be a sufficient force to defend the city against any army they could bring against it from the Virginia side of the Potomac.

The uncertainty, in my judgment, exists no longer. All evidence that has accumulated from various sources since we left Washington goes to prove most conclusively that almost the entire Rebel army in Virginia, amounting to not less than 120,000 men, is in the vicinity of Frederick City.

These troops, for the most part, consist of their oldest regiments, and are commanded by their best Generals. Several brigades joined them yesterday direct from Richmond, two deserters from which say that they saw no other troops between Richmond and Leesburg. Everything seems to indicate that they intend to hazard all upon the issue of the coming battle. They are probably aware that their forces are numerically superior to ours by at least twenty-five per cent. This, with the prestige of their recent successes, will, without doubt, inspire them with a confidence which will cause them to fight well. The momentous consequences involved in the struggle of the next few days impel me, at the risk of being considered slow and overcautious, to most earnestly recommend that every available man be at once added to this army.

I believe this army fully appreciates the importance of a victory at this time, and will fight well. But the result of a general battle, with such odds as the enemy now appears to have against us, might, to say the least, be doubtful; and if we should be defeated, the consequences to the country would be disastrous in the extreme. Under these circumstances, I would recommend that one or two of the three army corps now on the Potomac, opposite Washington, be at once withdrawn and sent to reinforce this army. I would also advise that the force of Colonel Miles, at Harper's Ferry, where it can be of but little use and is continually exposed to be cut off by the enemy, be immediately ordered here. This would add about twenty-five thousand old troops to our present force, and would greatly strengthen us.

If there are any Rebel forces remaining on the other side of the Potomac, they must be so few that the troops left in the forts, after two corps shall have been withdrawn, will be sufficient to check them; and with the large cavalry force now on that side kept well out on front to give warning of the distant approach of any very large army, a part of this army might be sent back within the entrenchments to assist in repelling an attack. But even if Washington should be taken while these armies are confronting each other, this would not, in my judgment, bear comparison with the ruin and disasters which would follow a signal defeat of this Army. If we should be successful in conquering the gigantic rebel army before us, we would have no difficulty in recovering it. On the other hand, should their force prove sufficiently powerful to defeat us, would all the forces now around Washington be sufficient to prevent such a victorious army from carrying the works this side of the Potomac, after they are uncovered by our Army? I think not.

From the moment the rebels commenced the policy of concentrating their forces, with their large masses of troops operating against our scattered forces, they have been successful. They are undoubtedly pursuing the same policy now, and are prepared to take advantage of any division of our troops in the future.

I therefore most respectfully, but strenuously urge upon you the absolute necessity, at this critical juncture, of uniting all our disposable forces. Every other consideration should yield to this; and if we defeat the army now arrayed before us, the rebellion is crushed; for I do not believe they can organize another army. But if we should be so unfortunate as to meet with defeat, our country is at their mercy."

McClellan to President Lincoln, 13 September 1862:

"I have the whole Rebel force in front of me but am confident and no time will be lost. I have a difficult task to perform but with God's blessing will accomplish it. I think Lee has made a gross mistake and that he will be severely punished for it. The Army is in motion as rapidly as possible. I hope for a great success if the plans of the Rebels remain unchanged...I have all the plans of the Rebels and will catch them in their own trap if my men are equal to the emergency. I now feel that I can count on them as of old..."

ORDER OF BATTLE
ARMY OF THE POTOMAC
MG George B. McClellan, U.S. Army, commanding
14-17 September 1862

On September 14 the right wing of the army, consisting of the First and Ninth Corps, was commanded by Major-General Burnside; the center, composed of the Second and Twelfth Corps, by Major-General Sumner; and the left wing, comprising the Sixth Corps and Couch's division (Fourth Corps), by Major-General Franklin.

FIRST ARMY CORPS (Maj. Gen. Joseph Hooker)
(Brig. Gen. George G. Meade)

First Division (Brig. Gen. Rufus King)
(Brig. Gen. John P. Hatch)
(Brig. Gen. Abner Doubleday)

First Brigade (Col. Walter Phelps, Jr.)
22d New York
24th New York
30th New York
84th New York (14th Militia)
2d U.S. Sharpshooters

Second Brigade (Brig. Gen. Abner Doubleday)
(Col. William P. Wainwright)
(Lieut. Col. J. William Hofmann)
7th Indiana
76th New York
95th New York
56th Pennsylvania

Third Brigade (Brig. Gen. Marsena R. Patrick)
21st New York
23d New York
35th New York
80th New York (20th Militia)

Fourth Brigade (Brig. Gen. John Gibbon)
19th Indiana
2d Wisconsin
6th Wisconsin
7th Wisconsin

Artillery (Capt. J. Albert Monroe)
New Hampshire Light, First Battery
1st Rhode Island Light, Battery D
1st New York Light, Battery L
4th United States, Battery B

Second Division (Brig. Gen. James B. Ricketts)

First Brigade (Brig. Gen. Abram Duryea)
- 97th New York
- 104th New York
- 105th New York
- 107th Pennsylvania

Second Brigade (Col. William A. Christian
(Col. Peter Lyle)
- 26th New York
- 94th New York
- 88th Pennsylvania
- 90th Pennsylvania

Third Brigade (Brig. Gen. George L. Hartsuff)
(Col. Richard Coulter)
- 12th Massachusetts
- 13th Massachusetts
- 83d New York (9th Militia)
- 11th Pennsylvania

Artillery
- 1st Pennsylvania Light, Battery F
- Pennsylvania Light, Battery C

Third Division (Brig. Gen. George G. Meade)
(Brig. Gen. Truman Seymour)

First Brigade (Brig. Gen. Truman Seymour)
(Col. R. Biddle Roberts)
- 1st Pennsylvania Reserves
- 2d Pennsylvania Reserves
- 5th Pennsylvania Reserves
- 6th Pennsylvania Reserves
- 13th Pennsylvania Reserves (1st Rifles)

Second Brigade (Col. Albert L. Magilton)
- 3d Pennsylvania Reserves
- 4th Pennsylvania Reserves
- 7th Pennsylvania Reserves
- 8th Pennsylvania Reserves

Third Brigade (Col. Thomas F. Gallagher)
(Lieut. Col. Robert Anderson)
- 9th Pennsylvania Reserves
- 10th Pennsylvania Reserves
- 11th Pennsylvania Reserves
- 12th Pennsylvania Reserves

Artillery
- 1st Pennsylvania Light, Battery A
- 1st Pennsylvania Light, Battery B
- 5th United States, Battery C

SECOND ARMY CORPS (Maj. Gen. Edwin V. Sumner)

First Division (Maj. Gen. Israel B. Richardson)
(Brig. Gen. John C. Caldwell)
(Brig. Gen. Winfield S. Hancock)

First Brigade (Brig. Gen. John C. Caldwell)
  5th New Hampshire
  7th New York
  61st New York
  64th New York
  81st Pennsylvania

Second Brigade (Brig. Gen. Thomas F. Meagher)
  (Col. John Burke)
  29th Massachusetts
  63d New York
  69th New York
  88th New York

Third Brigade (Col. John R. Brooke)
  2d Delaware
  52d New York
  57th New York
  66th New York
  53d Pennsylvania

Artillery
  1st New York Light, Battery B
  4th U.S., Batteries A and C

Second Division (Maj. Gen. John Sedgwick)
(Brig. Gen. Oliver O. Howard)

First Brigade (Brig. Gen. Willis A. Gorman)
  15th Massachusetts
  1st Minnesota
  34th New York
  82d New York (2d Militia)
  Massachusetts Sharpshooters, First Company
  Minnesota Sharpshooters, Second Company

Second Brigade (Brig. Gen. Oliver O. Howard)
  (Col. Joshua T. Owen)
  (Col. De Witt C. Baxter)
  69th Pennsylvania
  71st Pennsylvania
  72d Pennsylvania
  106th Pennsylvania

Third Brigade (Brig. Gen. Napoleon J. T. Dana)
  (Col. Norman J. Hall)
  19th Massachusetts
  20th Massachusetts
  7th Michigan
  42d New York
  59th New York

Artillery
  1st Rhode Island Light, Battery A
  1st United States, Battery I

24

Third Division (Brig. Gen. William H. French)

First Brigade (Brig. Gen. Nathan Kimball)
  14th Indiana
  8th Ohio
  132d Pennsylvania
  7th West Virginia

Second Brigade (Col. Dwight Morris)
  14th Connecticut
  108th New York
  130th Pennsylvania

Third Brigade (Brig. Gen. Max Weber)
(Col. John W. Andrews)
  1st Delaware
  5th Maryland
  4th New York

Unattached Artillery
  1st.New York Light, Battery G
  1st Rhode Island Light, Battery B
  1st Rhode Island Light, Battery G

FOURTH ARMY CORPS

First Division (Maj. Gen. Darius N. Couch)

First Brigade (Brig. Gen. Charles Devens, Jr.)
  7th Massachusetts
  10th Massachusetts
  36th New York
  2d Rhode Island

Second Brigade (Brig. Gen. Albion P. Howe)
  62d New York
  93d Pennsylvania
  98th Pennsylvania
  102d Pennsylvania
  139th Pennsylvania

Third Brigade (Brig. Gen. John Cochrane)
  65th New York
  67th New York
  122d New York
  23d Pennsylvania
  61st Pennsylvania
  82d Pennsylvania

Artillery
  New York Light, Third Battery
  1st Pennsylvania Light, Battery C
  1st Pennsylvania Light, Battery D
  2d United States, Battery G

FIFTH ARMY CORPS (Maj. Gen. Fitz John Porter)

First Division (Maj. Gen. George W. Morell)

First Brigade (Col. James Barnes)
- 2D MAINE
- 18th Massachusetts
- 22d Massachusetts
- 1st Michigan
- 13th New York
- 25th New York
- 118th Pennsylvania
- Massachusetts Sharpshooters, Second Company

Second Brigade (Brig. Gen. Charles Griffin)
- 2d District of Columbia
- 9th Massachusetts
- 32d Massachusetts
- 4th Michigan
- 14th New York
- 62d Pennsylvania

Third Brigade (Col. T. B. W. Stockton)
- 20th Maine
- 16th Michigan
- 12th New York
- 17th New York
- 44th New York
- 83d Pennsylvania
- Michigan Sharpshooters, Brady's company

Artillery
- Massachusetts Light, Battery C
- 1st Rhode Island Light, Battery C
- 5th United States, Battery D

Sharpshooters
- 1st United States

Second Division (Brig. Gen. George Sykes)

First Brigade (Lieut. Col. Robert C. Buchanan)
- 3d United States
- 4th United States
- 12th United States, First Battalion
- 12th United States, Second Battalion
- 14th United States, First Battalion
- 14th United States, Second Battalion

Second Brigade (Maj. Charles S. Lovell)
- 1st and 6th United States
- 2d and 10th United States
- 11th United States
- 17th United States

Third Brigade (Col. Gouverneur K. Warren)
- 5th New York
- 10th New York

Artillery
    1st United States, Batteries E and G
    5th United States, Battery I
    5th United States, Battery K

Artillery Reserve (Lieut. Col. William Hays)
    1st Battalion New York Light, Battery A
    1st Battalion New York Light, Battery B
    1st Battalion New York Light, Battery C
    1st Battalion New York Light, Battery D
    New York Light, Fifth Battery
    1st United States, Battery K
    4th United States, Battery G

SIXTH ARMY CORPS (Maj. Gen. William B. Franklin)

First Division (Maj. Gen. Henry W. Slocum)

First Brigade (Col. Alfred T. A. Torbert)
- 1st New Jersey
- 2d New Jersey
- 3d New Jersey
- 4th New Jersey

Second Brigade (Col. Joseph J. Bartlett)
- 5th Maine
- 16th New York
- 27th New York
- 96th Pennsylvania

Third Brigade (Brig. Gen. John Newton)
- 18th New York
- 31st New York
- 32d New York
- 95th Pennsylvania

Artillery (Capt. Emory Upton)
- Maryland Light, Battery A
- Massachusetts Light, Battery A
- New Jersey Light, Battery A
- 2d United States, Battery D

Second Division (Maj. Gen. William F. Smith)

First Brigade (Brig. Gen. Winfield S. Hancock)
(Col. Amasa Cobb)
- 6th Maine
- 43d New York
- 49th Pennsylvania
- 137th Pennsylvania
- 5th Wisconsin

Second Brigade (Brig. Gen. W. T. H. Brooks)
- 2d Vermont
- 3d Vermont
- 4th Vermont
- 5th Vermont
- 6th Vermont

Third Brigade (Col. William H. Irwin)
  7th Maine
  20th New York
  33d New York
  49th New York
  77th New York

Artillery (Capt. Romeyn B. Ayres)
  Maryland Light, Battery B
  New York Light, 1st Battery
  5th United States, Battery F

NINTH ARMY CORPS (Maj. Gen. Ambrose E. Burnside)
            (Maj. Gen. Jesse L. Reno)
            (Brig. Gen. Jacob D. Cox)

First Division (Brig. Gen. Orlando B. Willcox)

First Brigade (Col. Benjamin C. Christ)   Second Brigade (Col. Thomas Welsh)
  28th Massachusetts   8th Michigan*
  17th Michigan   46th New York
  79th New York   45th Pennsylvania
  50th Pennsylvania   100th Pennsylvania
  *Transferred from First Brigade
   September 16

Artillery
  Massachusetts Light, Eighth Battery
  2d United States, Battery E

Second Division (Brig. Gen. Samuel D. Sturgis)

First Brigade (Brig. Gen. James Nagle)   Second Brigade (Brig. Gen. Edward
  2d Maryland   Ferrero)
  6th New Hampshire   21st Massachusetts
  9th New Hampshire   35th Massachusetts
  48th Pennsylvania   51st New York
                                             51st Pennsylvania

Artillery
  Pennsylvania Light, Battery D
  4th United States, Battery E

Third Division (Brig. Gen. Isaac P. Rodman)

First Brigade (Col. Harrison S. Fairchild)   Second Brigade (Col. Edward Harland)
  9th New York   8th Connecticut
  89th New York   11th Connecticut
  103d New York   16th Connecticut
                                             4th Rhode Island

Artillery
  5th United States, Battery A

28

Kanawha Division (Brig. Gen. Jacob D. Cox)
(Col. Eliakim P. Scammon)

First Brigade (Col. Eliakim P. Scammon)
(Col. Hugh Ewing)
12th Ohio
23d Ohio
30th Ohio
Ohio Light Artillery, First Battery
Gilmore's company West Virginia
Cavalry
Harrison's company West Virginia
Cavalry

Second Brigade (Col. George Crook)
11th Ohio
28th Ohio
36th Ohio
Schambeck's company Chicago Dragoons
Kentucky Light Artillery, Simmonds'
battery

Unattached
6th New York Cavalry (eight companies)
Ohio Cavalry, Third Independent Company
3d U.S. Artillery, Batteries L and M

TWELFTH ARMY CORPS (Maj. Gen. Joseph K. F. Mansfield)
(Brig. Gen. Alpheus S. Williams)

First Division (Brig. Gen. Alpheus S. Williams)
(Brig. Gen. Samuel W. Crawford)
(Brig. Gen. George H. Gordon)

First Brigade (Brig. Gen. Samuel W.
Crawford)
(Col. Joseph F. Knipe)
10th Maine
28th New York
46th Pennsylvania
124th Pennsylvania
125th Pennsylvania
128th Pennsylvania

Third Brigade (Brig. Gen. George H.
Gordon)
(Col. Thomas H. Ruger)
27th Indiana
2d Massachusetts and Pennsylvania
Zouaves d'Afrique
13th New Jersey
107th New York
3d Wisconsin

Second Division (Brig. Gen. George S. Greene)

First Brigade (Lieut. Col. Hector
Tyndale)
(Maj. Orrin J. Crane)
5th Ohio
7th Ohio
66th Ohio
28th Pennsylvania

Second Brigade (Col. Henry J.
Stainrook)
3d Maryland
102d New York
111th Pennsylvania

Third Brigade (Col. William B. Goodrich)
(Lieut. Col. Jonathan Austin)
3d Delaware
Purnell Legion, Maryland
60th New York
78th New York

Artillery (Capt. Clermont L. Best)
Maine Light, 4th Battery
Maine Light, 6th Battery
1st New York Light, Battery M
New York Light, 10th Battery
Pennsylvania Light, Battery E
Pennsylvania Light, Battery F
4th United States, Battery F

CAVALRY DIVISION (Brig. Gen. Alfred Pleasonton)

First Brigade (Maj. Charles J. Whiting)
5th United States
6th United States

Third Brigade (Col. Richard H. Rush)
4th Pennsylvania
6th Pennsylvania

Second Brigade (Col. John F. Farnsworth)
8th Illinois
3d Indiana
1st Massachusetts
8th Pennsylvania

Fourth Brigade (Col. Andrew T. McReynolds)
1st New York
12th Pennsylvania

Fifth Brigade (Col. Benjamin F. Davis)
8th New York
3d Pennsylvania

Artillery
2d United States, Battery A
2d United States, Batteries B and L
2d United States, Battery M
3d United States, Batteries C and G

Unattached
15th Pennsylvania Cavalry (detachment), Col. William Palmer

ORDER OF BATTLE
ARMY OF NORTHERN VIRGINIA
GEN Robert E. Lee, C.S. Army, commanding
14-17 September 1862

LONGSTREET'S CORPS (Maj. Gen. James Longstreet)

McLaws' Division (Maj. Gen. Lafayette McLaws)

Kershaw's Brigade (Brig. Gen. J. B. Kershaw)
  2d South Carolina
  3d South Carolina
  7th South Carolina
  8th South Carolina

Semmes' Brigade (Brig. Gen. Paul J. Semmes)
  10th Georgia
  53d Georgia
  15th Virginia
  32d Virginia

Cobb's Brigade (Brig. Gen. Howell Cobb)
    (Lieut. Col. C. C. Sanders)
    (Lieut. Col. William MacRae)
  16th Georgia
  24th Georgia
  Cobb's (Georgia) Legion
  15th North Carolina

Barksdale's Brigade (Brig. Gen. William Barksdale)
  13th Mississippi
  17th Mississippi
  18th Mississippi
  21st Mississippi

Artillery (Maj. S. P. Hamilton)
    (Col. H. C. Cabell)
    Manly's (North Carolina) battery
    Pulaski (Georgia) Artillery
    Richmond (Fayette) Artillery
    Richmond Howitzers (1st company)
    Troup (Georgia) Artillery

Anderson's Division (Maj. Gen. Richard H. Anderson)

Wilcox's Brigade (Col. Alfred Cumming)
  8th Alabama
  9th Alabama
  10th Alabama
  11th Alabama

Armistead's Brigade (Brig. Gen. Lewis A. Armistead)
    (Col. J. G. Hodges)
  9th Virginia
  14th Virginia
  38th Virginia
  53d Virginia
  57th Virginia

Mahone's Brigade (Col. William A. Parham)
  6th Virginia
  12th Virginia
  16th Virginia
  41st Virginia
  61st Virginia

Pryor's Brigade (Brig. Gen. Roger A. Pryor)
  14th Alabama
  2d Florida
  8th Florida
  3d Virginia

Featherston's Brigade (Brig. Gen. Winfield S. Featherston)
   (Col. Carnot Posey)
  12th Mississippi
  16th Mississippi
  19th Mississippi
  2d Mississippi Battalion

Wright's Brigade (Brig. Gen. A. R. Wright)
  44th Alabama
  3d Georgia
  22d Georgia
  48th Georgia

Artillery (Maj. John S. Saunders)
  Donaldsonville (Louisiana) Artillery (Maurin's battery)
  Huger's (Virginia) battery
  Moorman's (Virginia) battery
  Thompson's (Grimes') (Virginia) battery

Jones' Division (Brig. Gen. David R. Jones)

Toombs' Brigade (Brig. Gen. Robert Toombs)
   (Col. Henry L. Benning)
  2d Georgia
  15th Georgia
  17th Georgia
  20th Georgia

Drayton's Brigade (Brig. Gen. Thomas F. Drayton)
  50th Georgia
  51st Georgia
  15th South Carolina

Kemper's Brigade (Brig. Gen. J. L. Kemper)
  1st Virginia
  7th Virginia
  11th Virginia
  17th Virginia
  24th Virginia

Anderson's Brigade (Col. George T. Anderson)
  1st Georgia (Regulars)
  7th Georgia
  8th Georgia
  9th Georgia
  11th Georgia

Artillery
  Wise (Virginia) Artillery (J. S. Brown's battery)

Pickett's Brigade (Col. Eppa Hunton)
  (Brig. Gen. R. B. Garnett)
  8th Virginia
  18th Virginia
  19th Virginia
  28th Virginia
  56th Virginia

Jenkins' Brigade (Col. Joseph Walker)
  1st South Carolina
  2d South Carolina Rifles
  5th South Carolina
  6th South Carolina
  4th South Carolina Battalion
  Palmetto (South Carolina) Sharp-shooters

Walker's Division (Brig. Gen. John G. Walker)

Walker's Brigade (Col. Van H. Manning)
(Col. E. D. Hall)
  3d Arkansas
  27th North Carolina
  46th North Carolina
  48th North Carolina
  30th Virginia
  French's (Virginia) battery

Ransom's Brigade (Brig. Gen. Robert Ransom, Jr.)
  24th North Carolina
  25th North Carolina
  35th North Carolina
  49th North Carolina
  Branch's Field Artillery (Virginia)

Hood's Division (Brig. Gen. John B. Hood)

Hood's Brigade (Col. W. T. Wofford)
  18th Georgia
  Hampton (South Carolina) Legion
  1st Texas
  4th Texas
  5th Texas

Law's Brigade (Col. E. M. Law)
  4th Alabama
  2d Mississippi
  11th Mississippi
  6th North Carolina

Artillery (Maj. B. W. Frobel)
  German Artillery (South Carolina)
  Palmetto Artillery (South Carolina)
  Rowan Artillery (North Carolina)

Evans' Brigade (Brig. Gen. Nathan G. Evans)
  -(Col. P. F. Stevens)
  17th South Carolina
  18th South Carolina
  22d South Carolina
  23d South Carolina
  Holcombe (South Carolina) Legion
  Macbeth (South Carolina) Artillery

ARTILLERY

Washington (Louisiana) Artillery (Col. J. B. Walton)
  1st Company
  2d Company
  3d Company
  4th Company

Lee's Battalion (Col. S. D. Lee)
  Ashland (Virginia) Artillery
  Bedford (Virginia) Artillery
  Brooks (South Carolina) Artillery
  Eubank's (Virginia) battery
  Madison (Louisiana) Light Artillery
  Parker's (Virginia) battery

JACKSON'S CORPS (Maj. Gen. Thomas J. Jackson)

Ewell's Division (Brig. Gen. A. R. Lawton)
(Brig. Gen. Jubal A. Early)

Lawton's Brigade (Col. M. Douglass)
   (Maj. J. H. Lowe)
   (Col. John H. Lamar)
   13th Georgia
   26th Georgia
   31st Georgia
   38th Georgia
   60th Georgia
   61st Georgia

Trimble's Brigade (Col. James A. Walker)
   15th Alabama
   12th Georgia
   21st Georgia
   21st North Carolina
   1st North Carolina Battalion

Early's Brigade (Brig. Gen. Jubal A. Early)
   (Col. William Smith)
   13th Virginia
   25th Virginia
   31st Virginia
   44th Virginia
   49th Virginia
   52d Virginia
   58th Virginia

Hay's Brigade (Brig. Gen. Harry T. Hays)
   5th Louisiana
   6th Louisiana
   7th Louisiana
   8th Louisiana
   14th Louisiana

Artillery (Maj. A. R. Courtney)
   Chesapeake (Maryland) Artillery
   Courtney (Virginia) Artillery
   Johnson's (Virginia) battery
   Louisiana Guard Artillery
   First Maryland Battery
   Staunton (Virginia) Artillery

Hill's Light Division (Maj. Gen. Ambrose P. Hill)

Branch's Brigade (Brig. Gen. L. O'B. Branch)
   (Col. James H. Lane)
   7th North Carolina
   18th North Carolina
   28th North Carolina
   33d North Carolina
   37th North Carolina

Archer's Brigade (Brig. Gen. J. J. Archer)
   (Col. Peter Turney)
   5th Alabama Battalion
   19th Georgia
   1st Tennessee (Provisional Army)
   7th Tennessee
   14th Tennessee

Gregg's Brigade (Brig. Gen. Maxcy Gregg)
   1st South Carolina (Provisional Army)
   1st South Carolina Rifles
   12th South Carolina
   13th South Carolina
   14th South Carolina

Pender's Brigade (Brig. Gen. William D. Pender)
   (Col. R. H. Brewer)
   16th North Carolina
   22d North Carolina
   34th North Carolina
   38th North Carolina

34

Field's Brigade (Colonel Brockenbrough)
  40th Virginia
  47th Virginia
  55th Virginia
  22d Virginia Battalion

Thomas' Brigade (Col. Edward L. Thomas)
  14th Georgia
  35th Georgia
  45th Georgia
  49th Georgia

Artillery (Maj. R. L. Walker)
  Crenshaw's (Virginia) battery
  Fredericksburg (Virginia) Artillery
  Letcher (Virginia) Artillery
  Pee Dee (South Carolina) Artillery
  Purcell (Virginia) Artillery

Jackson's Division (Brig. Gen. John R. Jones)
(Brig. Gen. W. E. Starke)
(Col. A. J. Grigsby)

Winder's Brigade (Col. A. J. Grigsby)
  (Lieut. Col. R. D. Gardner)
  (Maj. H. J. Williams)
  2d Virginia
  4th Virginia
  5th Virginia
  27th Virginia
  33d Virginia

Jones' Brigade (Col. B. T. Johnson)
  (Brig. Gen. J. R. Jones)
  (Capt. J. E. Penn)
  (Capt. A. C. Page)
  (Capt. R. W. Withers)
  21st Virginia
  42d Virginia
  48th Virginia
  1st Virginia Battalion

Taliaferro's Brigade (Col. E. T. H. Warren)
  (Col. J. W. Jackson)
  (Col. J. L. Sheffield)
  47th Alabama
  48th Alabama
  10th Virginia
  23d Virginia
  37th Virginia

Starke's Brigade (Brig. Gen. William E. Starke)
  (Col. L. A. Stafford)
  (Col. E. Pendleton)
  1st Louisiana
  2d Louisiana
  9th Louisiana
  10th Louisiana
  15th Louisiana
  Coppens' (Louisiana) battalion

Artillery (Maj. L. M. Shumaker)
  Alleghany (Virginia) Artillery
  Brockenbrough's (Maryland) battery
  Danville (Virginia) Artillery
  Hampden (Virginia) Artillery
  Lee (Virginia) Battery
  Rockbridge (Virginia) Artillery

Hill's Division (Maj. Gen. Daniel H. Hill)

Ripley's Brigade (Brig. Gen. Roswell S. Ripley)
(Col. George Doles)
4th Georgia
44th Georgia
1st North Carolina
3d North Carolina

Garland's Brigade (Brig. Gen. Samuel Garland, Jr.)
(Col. D. K. McRae)
5th North Carolina
12th North Carolina
13th North Carolina
20th North Carolina
23d North Carolina

Rodes' Brigade (Brig. Gen. R. E. Rodes)
3d Alabama
5th Alabama
6th Alabama
12th Alabama
26th alabama

Anderson's Brigade (Brig. Gen. George B. Anderson)
(Col. R. T. Bennett)
2d North Carolina
4th North Carolina
14th North Carolina
30th North Carolina

Colquitt's Brigade (Col. A. H. Colquitt)
13th Alabama
6th Georgia
23d Georgia
27th Georgia
28th Georgia

Artillery (Major Pierson)
Hardaway's (Alabama) battery
Jeff. Davis (Alabama) Artillery
Jones' (Virginia) battery
King William (Virginia) Artillery

RESERVE ARTILLERY (Brig. Gen. William N. Pendleton)

Brown's Battalion (Col. J. Thompson Brown)
Powhatan Artillery
Richmond Howitzers, 2d company
Richmond Howitzers, 3d company
Salem Artillery
Williamsburg Artillery

Jones' Battalion (Maj. H. P. Jones)
Morris (Virginia) Artillery
Orange (Virginia) Artillery
Turner's (Virginia) battery
Wimbish's (Virginia) battery

Cutts' Battalion (Lieut. Col. A. S. Cutts)
Blackshears' (Georgia) battery
Irwin (Georgia) Artillery
Lloyd's (North Carolina) battery
Patterson's (Georgia) battery
Ross's (Georgia) battery

Nelson's Battalion (Maj. William Nelson)
Amherst (Virginia) Artillery
Fluvanna (Virginia) Artillery
Huckstep's (Virginia) battery
Johnson's (Virginia) battery
Milledge (Georgia) Artillery

Miscellaneous
Cutshaw's (Virginia) battery
Dixie (Virginia) Artillery
Magruder (Virginia) Artillery
Rice's (Virginia) battery

CAVALRY (Maj. Gen. James E. B. Stuart)

Hampton's Brigade (Brig. Gen. Wade Hampton)
  1st North Carolina
  2d South Carolina
  10th Virginia
  Cobb's (Georgia) Legion
  Jeff. Davis Legion

Lee's Brigade (Brig. Gen. Fitz. Lee)
  1st Virginia
  3d Virginia
  4th Virginia
  5th Virginia
  9th Virginia

Robertson's Brigade (Brig. Gen. B. H. Robertson)
  (Col. Thomas T. Munford)
  2d Virginia
  6th Virginia
  7th Virginia
  12th Virginia
  17th Virginia Battalion

HORSE ARTILLERY (Capt. John Pelham)

  Chew's (Virginia) battery
  Hart's (South Carolina) battery
  Pelham's (Virginia) battery

ANTIETAM CASUALTIES

Estimates of numbers engaged in the battles of the Maryland Campaign vary, and statistics on killed, wounded, captured and missing are incomplete. Participants attempted to fill gaps as they wrote their official reports, and historians have tried to refine the data. The tabulation that follows is drawn from the Official Record, Vol. XIX, Pt. 1, pp. 189-20, 810-31, and from Thomas L. Livermore, Numbers and Losses in the Civil War in America, 1861-1865 (New York: Houghton, Mifflin and Company, 1901).

UNION ARMIES
Battles of South Mountain
14 September 1862
Total Engaged 28,480

	KILLED	WOUNDED	CAPTURED/MISSING	AGGREGATE
I Corps	170	720	43	933
VI Corps	115	416	2	533
IX Corps	158	670	30	858
Cav Bde	0	1	0	1
Total	443	1,807	75	2,325

Harpers Ferry
13-15 September 1862
Total Engaged 14,200

	KILLED	WOUNDED	CAPTURED/MISSING	AGGREGATE
Composite Garrison	44	173	12,520	12,737

38

Antietam
16-17 September 1862
Total Engaged 87,100

	KILLED	WOUNDED	CAPTURED/MISSING	AGGREGATE
I Corps	348	2,016	255	2,619
II Corps	860	3,801	548	5,209
V Corps	21	107	2	130
VI Corps	70	355	33	438
IX Corps	432	1,741	120	2,293
XII Corps	274	1,384	85	1,743
Couch's Div	0	9	0	9
Cav Div	5	23	0	28
Total	2,010	9,416	1,043	12,469

Boteler's Ford
19-20 September 1862

	KILLED	WOUNDED	CAPTURED/MISSING	AGGREGATE
V Corps	70	148	128/346	692

ARMY OF NORTHERN VIRGINIA
Total Killed and Wounded*
14-20 September 1862
Total Engaged 35,000

	KILLED	WOUNDED	AGGREGATE
Jackson's Corps	725	3,842	4,567
Longstreet's Corps	795	4,621	5,416
Evan's Independent Bde	47	262	309
Total	1,567	8,725	10,292

*Livermore estimates Confederate "Captured or Missing" to be approximately 2,000. Confederate returns in the Official Records do not address this category of losses and may underestimate killed and wounded.

ORGANIZATION

The infantry regiment was the basic administrative and tactical unit of Civil War armies. Regimental headquarters consisted of a colonel, lieutenant colonel, major, adjutant, quartermaster, surgeon (with rank of major), two assistant surgeons, a chaplain, sergeant major, quartermaster sergeant, commissary sergeant, hospital steward, and two principal musicians. Each company was staffed by a captain, a first lieutenant, a second lieutenant, a first sergeant, four sergeants, eight corporals, two musicians, and one wagoner.

The authorized strength of a Civil War infantry regiment was about 1,000 officers and men, arranged in ten companies plus a headquarters and (for the first half of the war at least) a band. Discharges for physical disability, disease, special assignments (bakers, hospital nurses, or wagoners), court martials, and battle injuries all combined to reduce effective combat strength. Before too long a typical regiment might be reduced to less than 500 troops.

Brigades were made up of two or more regiments, with four regiments being most common. Union brigades averaged 1,000 to 1,500 infantry, while a Confederate brigade averaged 1,500 to 1,800. Union brigades were designated by a number within their division, and each Confederate brigade was designated by the name of a current or former commander.

Divisions were formed of two or more brigades. Union divisions contained 2,500 to 4,000 infantry, while the Confederate infantry division was somewhat larger, containing 5,000 to 6,000 men. Union divisions were designated by a number within their corps, and Confederate divisions took the name of a current or former commander.

Corps were formed of two or more divisions. Two or more corps usually constituted an army, the largest operational organization. In the Eastern Theater, during the Maryland campaign, the principal adversaries were the Union Army of the Potomac and the Confederate Army of Northern Virginia. The Army of the Potomac was organized into six army corps and a cavalry division. Union artillery was organized into brigades of generally two to four batteries each, with each corps having one artillery brigade. The total number of Union troops present at Antietam was about 87,000, although a substantial lesser number were actually engaged.

The Army of Northern Virginia consisted of two infantry commands, or "wings", and a cavalry division. The right wing, commanded by Longstreet, contained five divisions and the left wing, commanded by Jackson, had four divisions. Confederate artillery was organized into brigades of about four to five batteries, each brigade assigned to a division. In addition, Longstreet's command had an artillery reserve of ten batteries and Jackson's command a reserve of fourteen batteries. Six additional batteries of horse artillery accompanied the cavalry. At the beginning of the campaign Lee's army numbered slightly less than 52,000 men. However, by the time the army had reached Sharpsburg the number was about 35,000.

CHART OF CIVIL WAR ARMY ORGANIZATION

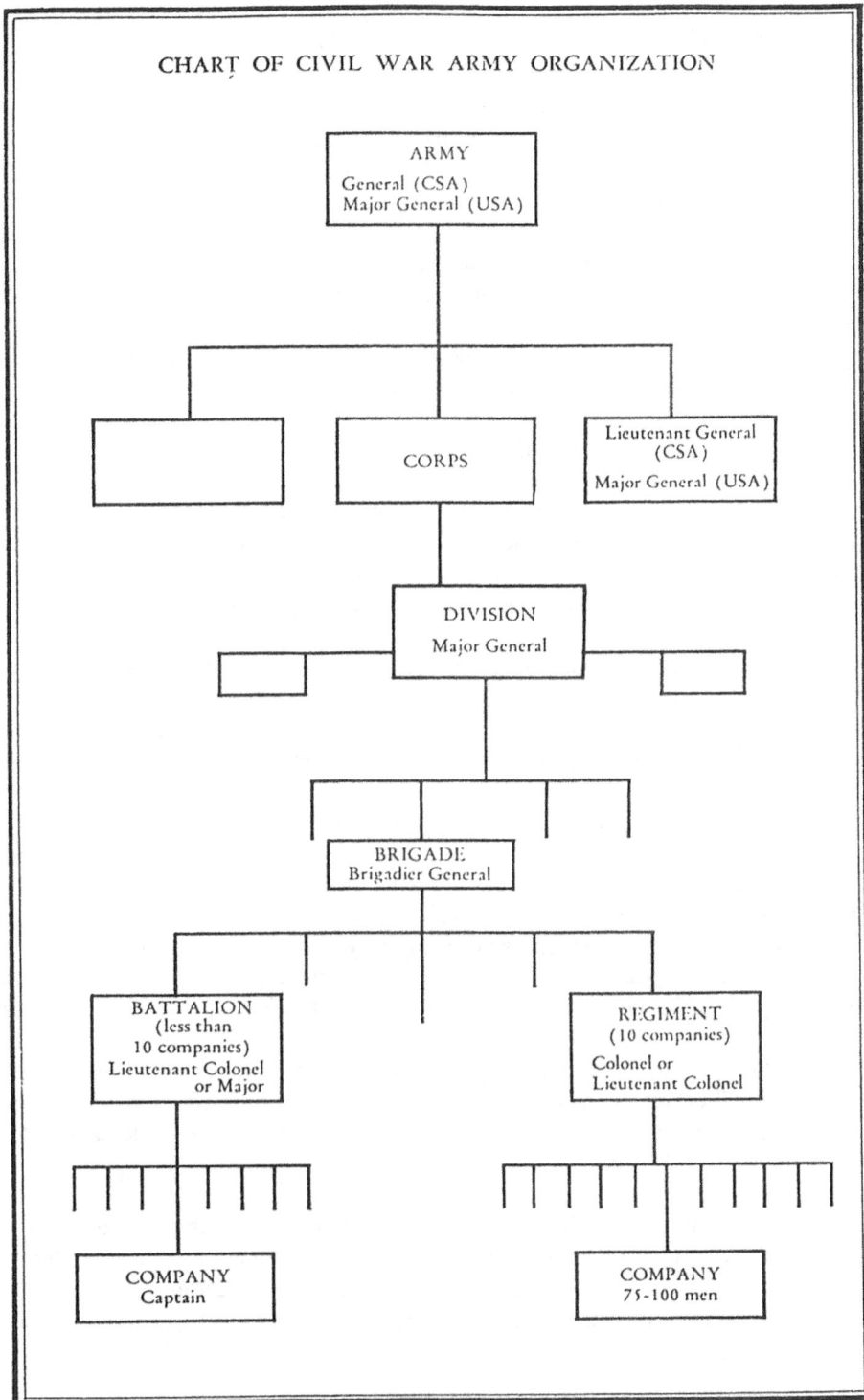

```
                    ┌─────────────────────────┐
                    │          ARMY           │
                    │     General (CSA)        │
                    │   Major General (USA)    │
                    └─────────────────────────┘
                                 │
          ┌──────────────────────┼──────────────────────┐
  ┌───────────────┐     ┌─────────────────┐     ┌─────────────────────────┐
  │               │     │      CORPS       │     │  Lieutenant General      │
  │               │     │                  │     │         (CSA)            │
  │               │     │                  │     │   Major General (USA)    │
  └───────────────┘     └─────────────────┘     └─────────────────────────┘
                                 │
                    ┌─────────────────────────┐
        ┌──────────┤        DIVISION          ├──────────┐
        │           │     Major General        │          │
  ┌──────────┐     └─────────────────────────┘     ┌──────────┐
  └──────────┘                                      └──────────┘
                                 │
          ┌──────────┬──────────┼──────────┬──────────┐
                    ┌─────────────────────────┐
                    │        BRIGADE           │
                    │    Brigadier General     │
                    └─────────────────────────┘
                                 │
      ┌─────────┬───────┬────────┼────────┬───────┬─────────┐
  ┌─────────────────┐                        ┌─────────────────────┐
  │    BATTALION     │                        │     REGIMENT         │
  │   (less than     │                        │   (10 companies)     │
  │  10 companies)   │                        │                      │
  │ Lieutenant Colonel│                       │     Colonel or       │
  │    or Major      │                        │  Lieutenant Colonel  │
  └─────────────────┘                        └─────────────────────┘
          │                                            │
  ┌┬┬┬┬┬┬┐                                   ┌┬┬┬┬┬┬┬┬┬┐
  ┌─────────────────┐                        ┌─────────────────────┐
  │    COMPANY       │                        │      COMPANY         │
  │    Captain       │                        │    75-100 men        │
  └─────────────────┘                        └─────────────────────┘
```

41

SMALL ARMS

In 1855 the U. S. Army adopted a .58 caliber rifled-musket to replace a .69 caliber smooth-bore musket. The new infantry arm was muzzle-loaded, its rifled barrel taking a hollow-based cylindro-conical bullet slightly smaller than the bore. Loading procedure required the soldier to withdraw a paper cartridge (containing powder and bullet) from his cartridge box, tear open one end with his teeth, pour the powder into the muzzle, place the bullet in the muzzle and ram it to the breech using a metal ramrod. A copper percussion cap was then placed on a hollow cone at the breech. To fire the weapon the hammer was cocked, and when the trigger was pulled the hammer struck the cap and ignited the powder charge. Each soldier was expected to be capable of loading and firing three aimed shots per minute. Although the maximum range of a rifled-musket might be over 1,000 yards actual fields of fire were often very short, the emphasis of musketry fire resting upon volume at close range rather than accuracy at long.

The basic ammunition load for each infantry soldier was 40 rounds in the cartridge box. When a large action was expected 20 additional rounds were issued to each soldier, who placed them in his uniform pockets or knapsack. In addition, 100 rounds per man were held in the brigade or division trains and 100 rounds in the corps trains.

At the beginning of the war a shortage of rifled-muskets on both sides forced the Northern and Southern governments to issue the older smooth-bore weapons, or purchase weapons from European nations. As the war progressed most soldiers eventually were armed with rifled-muskets, although even late in the war some troops on both sides still carried smooth-bores.

Before and during the war there were dozens of breech-loading rifles and carbines, both single and multiple-shot. Several types were purchased by the Government but were not issued in any numbers because of complicated construction, mechanical problems and cost. Three breech-loading rifles used by infantry were the .52 caliber, single-shot Sharps, .52 caliber, seven-shot Spencer, and .44 caliber fifteen-shot Henry. While the Sharps used a linen cartridge, the Spencer and Henry weapons used metallic, rimfire cartridges.

Handguns, both single and multiple shot, generally were generally carried by officers and possibly artillerymen. Although the types of handguns used by both sides were innumerable, two of the most common were six-shot revolvers produced by Colt and Remington, both in .36 and .44 caliber.

Union cavalry were initially armed with sabers and handguns, but soon added breech-loading carbines. In addition to Sharps and Spencer carbines, dozens of other types of breech-loaders, from .52 to .56 caliber, were issued. Confederate cavalrymen might be armed with a wide variety of handguns, shotguns, muzzle-loading carbines or captured Federal weapons.

TYPICAL CIVIL WAR SMALL ARMS

WEAPON	EFF. RANGE	RATE OF FIRE
U.S. rifled-musket, muzzle-loaded, cal .58	200-500 yds	3 rds/min
English Enfield rifled-musket, muzzle-loaded, cal .577	200-500 yds	3 rds/min
Smooth-bore musket, muzzle-loaded, cal .69	50-80 yds	3 rds/min
Henry rifle, fifteen-shot magazine, breech-loaded, cal .44	200-500 yds	16 rds/11 sec
Spencer carbine, seven-round magazine, breech-loaded, cal .52	150-200 yds	8 rds/20 sec
Sharps carbine, single-shot, breech-loaded, cal .52	150-200 yds	9 rds/min
Burnside carbine, single-shot, breech-loaded, cal .54	150-200 yds	9 rds/min
Revolvers, six-shot, cal .44	20-50 yds	

ARTILLERY

Civil War field artillery was organized into batteries of four or six guns. Regulations prescribed a captain as battery commander, while lieutenants commanded two-gun "sections." Each gun made up a platoon, under a sergeant ("chief of the piece") with 8 crewmen and six drivers.

During transportation each gun was attached to a limber, drawn by a six-horse team. The limber chest carried thirty to fifty rounds of ammunition, depending on the type of guns in the battery. In addition to the limbers, each gun had at least one caisson, also drawn by a six-horse team. The caisson carried additional ammunition in its two chests, as well as a spare wheel and tools. A horse-drawn forge and a battery wagon with tools accompanied each battery. A battery at full regulation strength, including all officers, noncoms, buglers, horse holders and other specialized functions, might exceed 100 officers and men. With spare horses included, a typical six-gun battery might have about 100-150 horses.

A battery could unlimber and fire an initial volley in about one minute, and each gun could continue firing two aimed shots a minute. The battery could limber up in about three minutes. Firing was by "direct fire," that is fire in which the target is in view of the gun. The prescribed distance between guns was fourteen yards from hub to hub. Therefore, a six-gun battery would represent a normal front of a little over 100 yards. Depth of the battery position, from the gun muzzle, passing the limber, to the rear of the caisson, was prescribed as 47 yards. In practice these measurements might be altered by terrain.

During firing cannoneers took their positions as in the diagram below. At the command "Commence firing," the gunner ordered "Load." While the gunner sighted the piece, Number 1 sponged the bore, Number 5 received a round from Number 7 at the limber and carried the round to Number 2, who placed it in the bore. Number 1 rammed the round to the breech while Number 3 "thumbed the vent." When the gun was loaded and sighted, Number 3 inserted a vent pick in the vent and punctured the cartridge bag. Number 4 attached a lanyard to a friction primer and inserted the primer in the vent. At the command "Fire," Number 4 yanked the lanyard. Number 6 cut fuses (if needed). The process was repeated until the command "Cease firing."

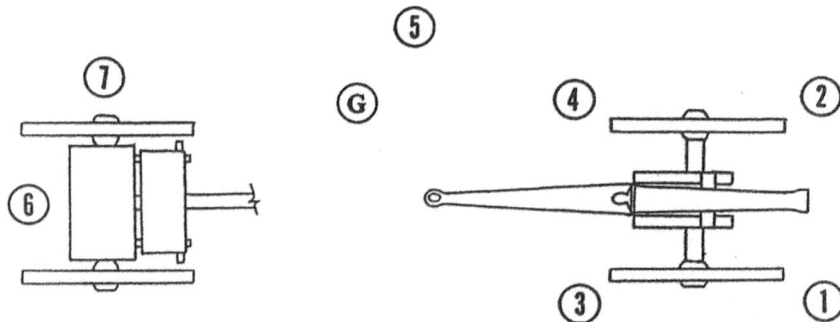

CIVIL WAR FIELD ARTILLERY - STATISTICS

WEAPON	TUBE COMPOSITION	EFF. RANGE
6-Pdr smooth-bore 3.67 in. bore	bronze	1500 yds
12-Pdr smooth-bore (Napoleon) 4.62 in. bore	bronze	1600 yds
10-Pdr rifle (Parrott) 3.00 in. bore*	iron	1800 yds
3-inch rifle (Ordnance) 3.00 in. bore	iron	1800 yds
20-Pdr rifle (Parrott) 3.67 in. bore	iron	1900 yds

Number of field guns at Antietam:

Union - 246 (Mostly 10-pounder Parrott and 3-inch Ordnance rifles)
Confederate - 293 (Mostly 6-pounder smooth-bores, 10-pounder Parrott and 3-inch Ordnance rifles)

*Caliber of Parrott M1861 is 2.9 in.; M1863 is 3.0 in.

ARTILLERY PROJECTILES

Four basic types of projectiles were employed by Civil War field artillery:

SHOT   BOLT

SOLID PROJECTILES - Round (spherical) projectiles of solid iron for smooth-bores were commonly called "cannonballs" or just plain "shot." When elongated for rifled weapons the projectile was known as a "bolt." Solid projectiles were used against opposing batteries, wagons, buildings, etc., as well as enemy personnel. While shot could ricochet across open ground against advancing infantry or cavalry, bolts tended to bury themselves upon impact with the ground and therefore were not used a great deal by field artillery.

SPHERICAL SHELL   RIFLED SHELL

SHELL - The shell, whether spherical or conical, was a hollow iron projectile filled with a black powder bursting charge. It was designed to break into several ragged fragments. Spherical shells exploded by fuses set into an opening in the shell, and were ignited by the flame of the cannon's propelling charge. The time of detonation was determined by adjusting the length of the fuse. Conical shells were detonated by similar timed fuses, or by impact. Shells were intended to impact on the target.

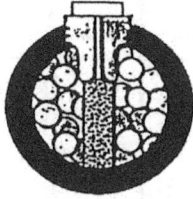

SPHERICAL CASE SHOT

RIFLED CASE SHOT

CASE SHOT - Case shot, or "shrapnel" was the invention of Henry Shrapnel, an English artillery officer. The projectile had a thinner wall than a shell and was filled with a number of small lead or iron balls (27 for a 12-pounder). A timed fuse ignited a small bursting charge which fragmented the casing and scattered the contents in the air. Case shot was intended to burst from fifty to seventy-five yards short of the target, the fragments being carried forward by the velocity of the shot.

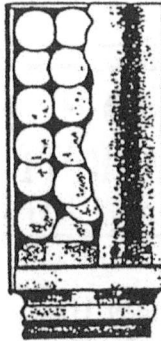

CANISTER

CANISTER - Canister consisted of a tin cylinder in which was packed a number of iron or lead balls. Upon discharge the cylinder split open and the smaller projectiles fanned out. Canister was an extremely effective anti-personnel weapon, with a maximum range of 400 yards. In emergencies double loads of canister could be used at ranges less than 200 yards, using a single propelling charge.

TABLE OF FIRE. LIGHT 12-POUNDER GUN. MODEL 1857.

SHOT. Charge 2½ Pounds.		SPHERICAL CASE SHOT. Charge 2½ Pounds.			SHELL. Charge 2 Pounds.		
ELEVATION In Degrees.	RANGE In Yards.	ELEVATION In Degrees.	TIME OF FLIGHT. Seconds.	RANGE In Yards.	ELEVATION In Degrees.	TIME OF FLIGHT In Seconds.	RANGE In Yards.
0°	323	0°50'	1"	300	0°	0"75	300
1°	620	1°	1"75	575	0°30	1"25	425
2°	875	1°30'	2"5	635	1°	1"75	615
3°	1200	2°	3"	730	1°30'	2"25	700
4°	1325	3°	4"	960	2°	2"75	785
5°	1680	3°30'	4"75	1080	2°30'	3"5	925
		3°40'	5"	1135	3°	4"	1080
					3°45'	5"	1300

Use SHOT at masses of troops, and to batter, from 600 up to 2.000 yards. Use SHELL for firing buildings, at troops posted in woods, in pursuit, and to produce a moral rather than a physical effect; greatest effective range 1,500 yards. Use SPHERICAL CASE SHOT at masses of troops, at not less than 500 yards; generally up to 1,500 yards. CANISTER is not effective at 600 yards; it should not be used beyond 500 yards, and but very seldom and over the most favorable ground at that distance; at short ranges, (less than 200 yards,) in emergency. use double canister, with single charge. Do not employ RICOCHET at less distance than 1,000 to 1,100 yards.

CARE OF AMMUNITION CHEST.

1st. Keep everything out that does not belong in them, except a bunch of cord or wire for breakage; beware of loose tacks, nails, bolts, or scraps.
2d. Keep friction primers in their papers, tied up. The pouch containing those for instant service must be closed, and so placed as to be secure. Take every precaution that primers do not get loose; a single one may cause an explosion. Use plenty of tow in packing.

(This sheet is to be glued on to the inside of Limber Chest Cover.)

TABLE OF FIRE
20-PDR. PARROTT GUN
Charge, 2 lbs. of Mortar Powder

ELEVATION In Degrees	PROJECTILE		RANGE In Yards	TIME OF FLIGHT In Seconds
1	Case Shot,	19½ lbs.	620	1⅞
2	Case Shot,	19½ lbs.	950	3⅛
3⅝	Shell,	18¾ lbs.	1500	4¾
5	Shell,	18¾ lbs.	2100	6½
10	Shell,	18¾ lbs.	3350	11¼
15	Shell,	18¾ lbs.	4400	17¼

CARE OF AMMUNITION CHEST

1st. Keep everything out that does not belong in them, except a bunch of cord or wire for breakage; beware of loose tacks, nails, bolts, or scraps.
2nd. Keep friction primers in their papers, tied up. The pouch containing those for instant service must be closed, and so placed as to be secure. Take every precaution that primers do not get loose; a single one may cause an explosion. Use plenty of tow in packing.

(This sheet is to be glued to the inside of Limber Chest Cover.)

Firing tables were glued to the inside of limber ammunition chest lids.

TACTICS

The tactical legacy of the eighteenth century had emphasized close order formations of soldiers trained to maneuver in concert and fire by volleys. These "linear" tactics stressed the tactical offensive. Assault troops advanced in line, two ranks deep, with cadenced steps, stopping to fire volleys on command and finally rushing the last few yards to pierce the enemy line with a bayonet charge.

These tactics were adequate for troops armed with single-shot, muzzle-loading, smooth-bore muskets with an effective range of about eighty yards. The close-order formation was therefore necessary to concentrate the fire power of these inaccurate weapons. Bayonet charges might then succeed because infantry could rush the last eighty yards before the defending infantrymen could reload their muskets after firing a volley.

The U.S. Army's transition from smooth-bore muskets to rifled-muskets in the mid-nineteenth century would have two main effects in the American Civil War: it would strengthen the tactical defensive and increase the number of casualties in the attacking force. With a weapon which could cause casualties out to 1,000 yards defenders firing rifles could decimate infantry formations attacking according to linear tactics.

During the Civil War the widespread use of the rifled-musket caused infantry assault formations to loosen up somewhat, with individual soldiers seeking available cover and concealment. However, because officers needed to maintain visual and verbal control of their commands during the noise, smoke and chaos of combat, close-order tactics to some degree would continue to the end of the war.

A typical combat formation of a regiment might be six companies in the main line, with two in reserve, and two out in front in extended skirmish order. During battle additional companies might be fed into the skirmish line, or the skirmishers might regroup on the main line.

Rapid movement of units on roads or cross country, was generally by formation of a column four men abreast. The speed of such columns was prescribed as 2 miles per hour. Upon reaching the field each regiment was typically formed into a line two ranks deep, the shoulders of each man in each rank touching the shoulders of the man on either side. The distance beween ranks was prescribed as thirteen inches. A regiment of 500 men (250 men in each rank), might have a front of about 200 yards. Both front and rear ranks were capable of firing, either by volley or individual fire.

Legend:

CPT □ 2LT □

1SG ⊠ 1LT □

Adjutant □

LTC

COL

Junior Major □

Band □

Senior Major □

Sergeant Major □

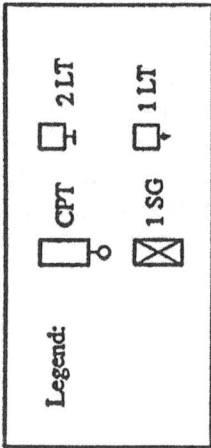

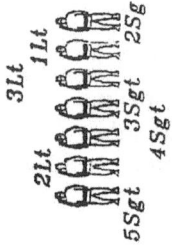

File Closers
(positioned behind each company)

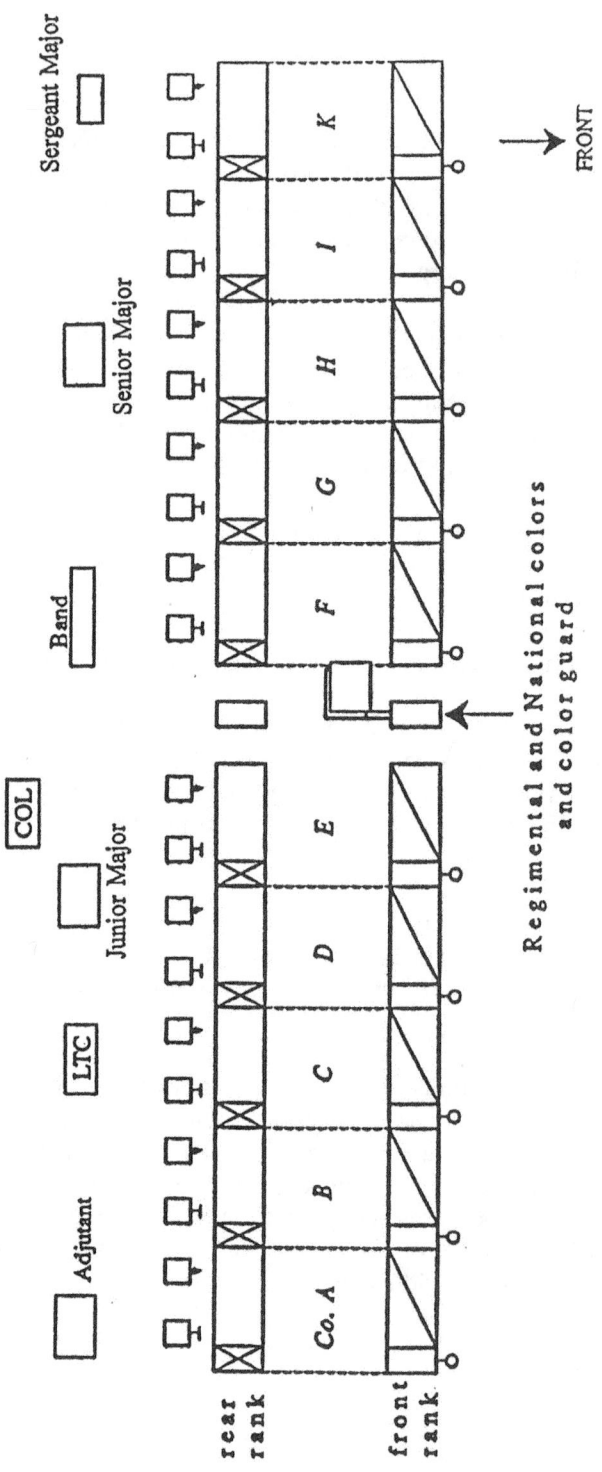

3Lt 1Lt
2Lt 3Sgt 2Sg
5Sgt 4Sgt

Co. A   B   C   D   E   F   G   H   I   K

rear rank

front rank

Regimental and National colors and color guard

FRONT

Regiment Formed Into Line of Battle

50

LOGISTICS

BUREAU SYSTEM. Bureau chiefs and heads of staff departments were responsible for various aspects of the Army's administration and logistics and reported directly to the Secretary of War. The division of responsibility and authority over them among the Secretary of War, the Assistant Secretaries, and the General in Chief was never spelled out, and the supply departments functioned independently and without effective coordination throughout most of the Civil War, although much improved after Grant took command.

Logistical support was entrusted to the heads of four supply departments in Washington: the Quartermaster General, responsible for clothing and equipment, forage, animals, transportation, and housing; the Commissary General for rations; the Chief of Ordnance for weapons, ammunition, and miscellaneous related equipment; and the Surgeon General for medical supplies, evacuation, treatment, and hospitalization of the wounded.

For other support there were the Adjutant General, the Inspector General, the Paymaster General, the Judge Advocate General, the Chief of Engineers, and the Chief of Topographical Engineers.

The military department was the basic organizational unit for administrative and logistical purposes, and the commander of each department controlled the support in that area with no intervening level between his departmental headquarters and the bureau chiefs in Washington. There were six departments when the war started (East, West, Texas, New Mexico, Utah, and Pacific); however, later on, boundaries changed and several geographical departments might be grouped together as a military "division" headquarters.

Army depots were located in major cities: Boston, New York, Baltimore, Washington, Cincinnati, Louisville, St. Louis, Chicago, New Orleans, and San Francisco. Philadelphia was the chief depot and manufacturing center for clothing. Advanced and temporary supply bases were established as needed to support active operations. Until 1864 most depots were authorized the rank of captain as commander, who despite their low rank and meager pay, had tremendous resources of men, money, and material under their control. There were a few exceptions, notably COL Daniel H. Rucker at the Washington QM Depot and COL George D. Ramsay at the Washington Arsenal. The primary function of the depots was to procure supplies and prepare them for use in the field by repacking, assembling, or other similar tasks.

Procurement was decentralized. Purchases were made on the market by low-bid contract in the major cities and producing areas by depot officers. Flour and some other commodities were procured closer to the troops when possible. Cattle were contracted for at specific points, and major beef depots were maintained at Washington (on the grounds of the unfinished Washington Monument), Alexandria, VA, and Louisville, KY. The Subsistence Department developed a highly effective system of moving cattle on the hoof to the immediate rear of the armies in the field, to be slaughtered by brigade butchers and issued to the troops the day before consumption.

The Confederate Army used a similar system with depots at Richmond, Staunton, Raleigh, Atlanta, Columbus (GA), Huntsville, Montgomery, Jackson (MS), Little Rock, Alexandria (LA), and San Antonio.

SUPPLY OPERATIONS. Most unit logistics were accomplished at regimental level. The regimental QM was normally a line lieutenant designated by the regimental commander. His duties included submitting requisitions for all QM supplies and transport, accounting for regimental property including tentage, camp equipment, extra clothing, wagons, forage, and animals; issuing supplies and managing the regimental trains. The regimental commissary officer, also designated from the line, requisitioned, accounted for, and issued rations. The regimental ordnance officer had similar duties regarding arms and ammunition and managed the movement of the unit ammunition train.

In theory, logistical staff positions above the regiment were filled by a fully qualified officer of the supply department concerned, However, experienced officers were in perpetual short supply, and many authorized positions were filled by officers and noncommissioned officers from line units or left vacant, the duties performed by someone in addition to their own. This problem existed in both armies, where inexperience and ignorance of logistical principles and procedures generally reduced levels of support.

The Soldier's Load: About 45 lbs. (Union) - Musket and bayonet (14 lbs.), 60 rounds, 3-8 days rations, canteen, blanket or overcoat, shelter half, ground sheet, mess gear (cup, knife, fork, spoon, skillet), personal items (sewing kit, razor, letters, Bible, etc.). Confederates usually had less, about 30 lbs.

Official US Ration: 20 oz. of fresh or salt beef or 12 oz. of pork or bacon, 18 oz. of flour or 20 of corn meal (bread in lieu if possible), 1.6 oz. of rice or .64 oz. of beans or 1.5 oz of dried potatoes, 1.6 oz of coffee or .24 oz. of tea, 2.4 oz. of sugar, .54 oz. of salt, .32 gill of vinegar.

Union Marching Ration: 16 oz. of "hardtack," 12 oz. salt pork or 4 oz. fresh meat, 1 oz. coffee, 3 oz. sugar, and salt.

Confederate Ration: Basically the same but with slightly more sugar and less meat, coffee, vinegar and salt, and seldom issued in full. For the Army of Northern Virginia usually half of meat issued and coffee available only when captured or exchanged through the lines for sugar and tobacco. During the Maryland campaign foraging was disappointing, so Confederate soldiers supplemented the issue ration with corn from the fields and fruit from the orchards.

Forage: Each horse required 14 lbs. of hay and 12 of grain per day; mules needed the same amount of hay and 9 lbs of grain. No other item was so bulky and difficult to transport.

Union Annual Clothing Issue: 2 caps, 1 hat, 2 dress coats, 3 pr. trousers, 3 flannel shirts, 3 flannel drawers, 4 pr. stockings and 4 pr. bootees (high top shoes). Artillerymen and cavalrymen were issued jackets and boots instead of bootees. Allowance = $42.

Confederate: Officially, the Confederate soldier was almost equally well clothed, but the QM was seldom able to supply the required items and soldiers wore whatever came to hand, the home-dyed butternut jackets and trousers being characteristic items. Shortages of shoes were a constant problem.

Tents: Sibley (tepee) held 20 men feet to center pole; early in war Union introduced the tente de'Abri (shelter half), used by the French Army, and called "dog" tent by witty soldiers, now pup tent.

Baggage: Enlisted men of both armies were required to carry their own. Union order of Sep 1862 limited officers to blankets, one small valise or carpet bag and an ordinary mess kit. Confederate standards allowed generals 80 lbs., field officers 65 lbs., and captains and subalterns 50 lbs.

Wagons: Union's standard 6-mule Army wagon could haul 4,000 lbs on good roads in the best of conditions but seldom exceeded 2,000 or with 4 mules 1,800 lbs. at rate of 12-24 miles a day. Confederates often used 4-mule wagon with smaller capacity.
Army of the Potomac authorized wagons as follows:

corps hq	4
div and bde hq	3
regt of Inf	6
arty bty and cav	3

One wagon per regiment was reserved for hospital stores and one for grain for officers' horses.

The Army of Northern Virginia used 4-mule wagons as follows:

div hq	3
bde hq	2
regt hq	1
regt's medical stores	1
regt's ammunition	1

1/100 men per regt for baggage, camp equipment, rations, etc.

Numbers of supply wagons per 1,000 men:

Army of the Potomac (1862)	29
Jackson in the Valley (1862)	7
Army of Northern Virginia (1863)	28
Army of the Potomac (1864)	36
Sherman's March to the Sea (1864)	40
Napoleon's standard	12.5

1862	EAST	WEST
JAN.		HENRY AND DONELSON CAMPAIGN
FEB.	PENINSULAR CAMPAIGN	⌐Fort Henry └Fort Donelson SHILOH CAMPAIGN
MAR.	⌐Troops Embark	⌐Battle of └Pea Ridge
APR.	Siege of Yorktown VALLEY CAMPAIGN	└Shiloh STONES RIVER CAMPAIGN ⌐Capture of └New Orleans
MAY	Seven Pines ⌐McDowell ‑Winchester	
JUNE	Seven Days Battles ‑Port Republic └Jackson Leaves the Valley	‑Corinth Captured ‑Buell Starts	Combined Fleet and Land Operations Against Vicksburg
JULY	2D BULL RUN CAMPAIGN	‑Buell Halted
AUG.	└Withdrawal ANTIETAM CAMPAIGN ‑Cedar Mountain ‑2d Bull Run	Kirby Smith Starts North Bragg Starts North
SEPT.	⌐Antietam	⌐Buell at └Louisville GRANT'S FIRST ADVANCE ON VICKSBURG
OCT.	FREDERICKSBURG CAMPAIGN	‑Perryville ⌐Corinth
NOV.	‑McClellan Relieved	‑Buell Relieved
DEC.	⌐Fredericksburg	‑Rosecrans at Nashville └Stones River	‑Grant Reaches Oxford ‑Holly Springs Chickashaw └Bluffs

UNITED STATES IN 1861

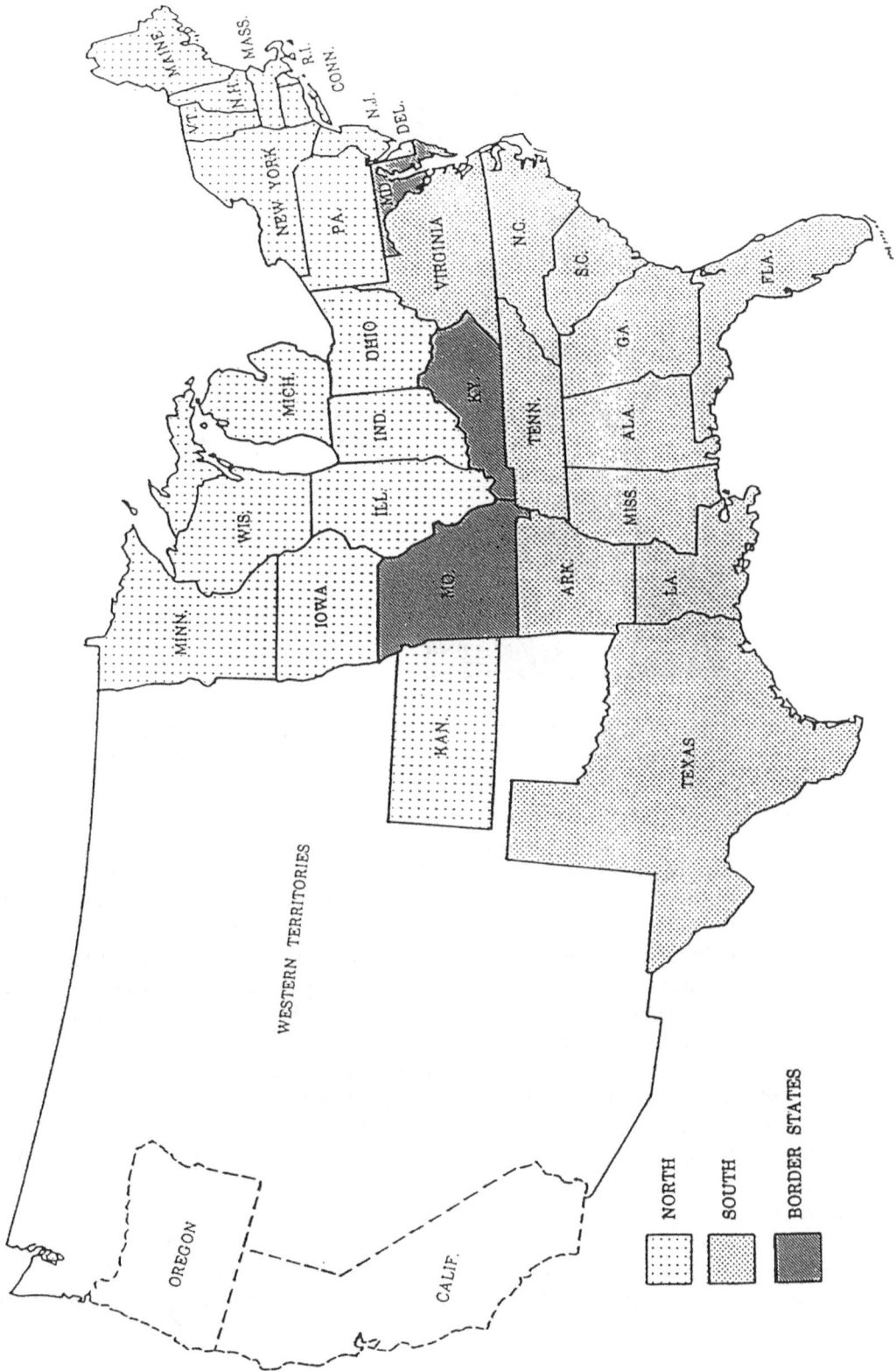

MAINE

VT. N.H. MASS.

R.I.

CONN.

N.Y.

NEW YORK

N.J.

PA.

DEL.

MD.

OHIO

VIRGINIA

N.C.

MICH.

IND.

KY.

S.C.

TENN.

GA.

WIS.

ILL.

ALA.

FLA.

MINN.

IOWA

MO.

MISS.

ARK.

LA.

KAN.

TEXAS

WESTERN TERRITORIES

OREGON

CALIF.

NORTH

SOUTH

BORDER STATES

SELECTED BIOGRAPHICAL SKETCHES
OF UNION LEADERS

LINCOLN, Abraham
1809-1865, Kentucky

Lincoln was born in Kentucky and raised on the edge of the frontier, growing up with scant formal education. His family then settled in Illinois, where Lincoln held various clerking jobs, and was partner in a grocery store that failed and left him heavily in debt. He studied law and his forceful character and honesty made him a favorite in the community and elected him to the state legislature as a Whig. Licensed as a lawyer in 1836, he settled in Springfield and became a successful and well-known attorney. He married Mary Todd in 1842. After serving one term in Congress (1847-49) he was not returned by his constituents and retired from public life.

In opposition to Stephen A. Douglas and the Kansas-Nebraska Act, Lincoln entered into the growing debate of sectionalism, joining the Republican party in 1856. Although the famous Lincoln-Douglas debates of 1858 ended in Douglas' election to the Senate, Lincoln emerged as a powerful national figure. He gained the Republican nomination for President and after his election on 6 Nov 1860 the South saw the end of their political power in the Union, and southern states began seceding. When Southern forces attacked the Federal garrison at Fort Sumter, S.C., in Apr 1861, Lincoln called upon the various states to furnish volunteers to put down the rebellion. Frequently advised by governors and congressmen, Lincoln selected many generals from among leading politicians in order to give himself a broader base of political support. Some political generals, such as John A. Logan and Francis P. Blair, distinguished themselves, whereas others proved military hindrances. Other commissions were given to Regulars on active duty, former West Pointers like George B. McClellan and Ambrose Burnside, who had resigned to pursue business careers, or those who had held volunteer commissions in the Mexican War.

During the war Lincoln appointed and discarded a secession of commanding generals as he was subjected to repeated humiliation in the defeat of Union arms. After McDowell's defeat at First Manassas in Jul 1861, Lincoln appointed McClellan commander-in-chief of all armies, and acquiesced in that commander's oblique movement with the Army of the Potomac against Richmond via the Peninsula. After this unsuccessful campaign, however, Lincoln relieved McClellan of supreme command, allowing him to retain command of the Army of the Potomac, and placed John Pope in command of a separate Army of Virginia.

After Pope's defeat at Second Manassas (29-30 Aug 1862) Lincoln reconsolidated both armies under McClellan, who led the hastily assembled force to block Lee's invasion of Maryland.

Earlier, Lincoln had drafted a proclamation freeing slaves in the rebellious states but withheld it because, after Union reverses, it might appear an act of desperation. When McClellan's army successfully halted Lee at Antietam (17 Sep 1862), the Emancipation Proclamation was issued, changing the war's focus (heretofore fought to preserve the Union and not to disrupt the South's social fabric) to include ending slavery.

When McClellan failed to actively pursue Lee after Antietam Lincoln relieved him. The failure of McClellan's successors - Burnside at Fredericksburg (13 Dec 1862) and Hooker at Chancellorsville (1-4 May 1863) - added to Lincoln's perplexity and tended to discredit his ability in military matters. Meade's success at Gettysburg (1-3 Jul 1863) was marred by the failure to pursue and crush Lee's army. Even under Grant, whom Lincoln brought East in the spring of 1864, there were months of sanguinary fighting with hope deferred.

Lincoln's political enemies mustered strength before the 1864 election, and it looked as though he would be displaced in the White House by Democratic challenger George B. McClellan. But the military successes of Grant's overland campaign and Sherman's capture of Atlanta swung sentiment to him, and Lincoln was re-elected. He was assassinated by John Wilkes Booth on 14 Apr '65 at Ford's Theater, Washington, five weeks after his second inauguration and five days after Lee's surrender.

STANTON, Edwin McMasters
1814-1869, Ohio

In 1827 Stanton's father died, forcing the 13-year-old to leave school and work in a bookstore to supplement the family's income. He studied law in Columbus and was admitted to the bar in 1836. From 1849 to 1856 he was counsel for the state of Pennsylvania, establishing a national reputation. In 1859 he successfully defended Congressman Daniel Sickles in a celebrated Washington murder case, and in the waning days of the Buchanan administration he was appointed attorney general.

Nominally a Democrat, Stanton backed John C. Breckinridge in the election of 1860, and after Lincoln was inaugurated he returned to private life. In Jan 1862 Lincoln offered him the position of secretary of war, which he accepted, sacrificing a yearly income of $40,000 as a successful lawyer for a cabinet post of $8,000.

With no military experience, he moved into office with zeal, fighting fraud and waste in the rapidly enlarged military. A capable organizer, he brought order out of chaos. He generally worked well with congressional leaders and generals in the field. However, when George McClellan, a personal friend, failed to perform adequately Stanton was one of the leading forces pushing for his removal. His manner and restrictions on the press earned him few friends and later led to some apparently unfounded charges that he was involved in the assassination of Lincoln.

After the war Stanton worked with the Radical Republicans in their efforts to secure harsher treatment for the South. This brought him into conflict with his new president, Andrew Johnson. Matters came to a head in 1868 when the president removed him from office. Congress reinstated him under the Tenure of Office Act but Johnson persisted, naming Grant as secretary of war. Stanton, however, barricaded himself in his office and Grant, supportive of Stanton, refused to take office. The crisis ended on 26 May 1868 when Stanton finally resigned and resumed his legal practice.

In Dec 1869, on Grant's election to the presidency, Stanton was named to the U.S. Supreme Court, but died four days after Congress confirmed the nomination.

HALLECK, Henry W.
1815-1872, New York
USMA 1839 (3/31); Engrs.

After graduating from West Point Halleck was assigned to work on the fortifications in New York Harbor, then toured Europe and inspecting fortifications. Afterwards he was invited by the Lowell Institute of Boston to deliver a series of twelve lectures on the elements of military art and science. When the Mexican War broke out Halleck, then a first lieutenant, was assigned to Monterey, California, where he filled varied and responsible positions. He was brevetted captain for gallantry "in affairs with the enemy" on 1 May '47. After the war he was an inspector and engineer of light-houses and acted a member of a board of engineers for fortifications on the Pacific Coast. He was promoted captain 1 Jul '53 but because of cuts in the army after the war and the hopeless future in a profession little rewarded by the government, he resigned 1 Aug 54. The same year he became head of the leading law firm in California, refusing offers to run for the U.S. Senate. He later became director of the New Almaden quick-silver mine and a major general of California militia.

At the beginning of the Civil War he was commissioned major general in the R.A. (19 Aug '61), and commanded the Department of the Missouri. The success of his subordinates, Grant and Foote at Donelson, Curtis at Pea Ridge, Pope at Island No. 10, and Grant at Shiloh, brought prestige to Halleck's department. The departments of Kansas and Ohio were added to his command on 11 Mar '62, and the whole named the Department of the Mississippi. Halleck then took to the field in person. Although his army had double the number of his opponent's forces, Halleck's labors in the field were not so meritorious as in the office. Though he captured Corinth he allowed the enemy's forces to escape and failed to pursue them with vigor. This movement ended Halleck's active campaigning, during which he was known to the soldiers as "Old Brains."

On 11 Jul '62, he was summoned to Washington and made military advisor to the President with the title of general-in-chief. Brusque, mathematical, direct, wholly impersonal and impartial, Halleck not only antagonized office seekers and politicians but also his subordinates far away in the field. His counsels to his generals were frequent and often superfluous and he devoted much of his time to minutiae and the manner of raising soldiers and equipment.

On 12 Mar '64, after Grant was promoted to lieutenant general, Halleck's status was changed from general-in-chief to chief of staff. Although the new office was more logical and appropriate to the work Halleck had been doing, it nevertheless was a demotion. Unlike other generals, who asked to be relieved or reassigned when they could not have positions to which they believed themselves entitled, Halleck pursued his duties with his same unflagging energy. On 19 Apr '65, after Appomattox, he was relieved from the office of chief of staff and three days later assigned to command the Military Division of the James, with headquarters in Richmond. On 30 August he was transferred to command the Military Division of the Pacific with headquarters at San Francisco and on 16 Mar '69 he was placed in command of the Division of the South, at Louisville, Ky., his last assignment before his death.

McCLELLAN, George B.
1826-1885, Pennsylvania
USMA 1846 (2/59); Engrs.

During the Mexican War McClellan won three brevets for gallant and meritorious conduct, and later spent a year in Europe observing foreign military methods. He resigned in 1857 as a capt. and entered the railroad business, first with the Illinois Central, then with the Ohio and Mississippi. McClellan started the war as a maj. gen. of Ohio volunteers and was soon made maj. gen. in the R.A. and given command of the Dept. of the Ohio. His success in a minor victory at Rich Mountain, W.Va., just 10 days before the Federal disaster at First Manassas (21 Jul '61), put him in the public eye at a critical time.

Given command of the armies around Washington (later known as the Army of the Potomac) and later succeeding Gen. Scott as CG of the Army 1 Nov '61), he undertook with marked success the complex task of organizing and training the Union armies. In the spring of 1862 the "Young Napoleon," as he was being called, took the Army of the Potomac to the Virginia Peninsula to capture Richmond. McClellan vastly overestimated the forces opposing him during the campaign, blamed Washington for lack of support and refused to resume the offensive until given reinforcements. Instead, Lincoln ordered the Army of the Potomac north to join John Pope's Army of Virginia - a force organized to move against Richmond via the line of the Orange and Alexandria R.R. Before all of McClellan's forces could join Pope the Army of Virginia was defeated at Second Manassas (29-30 Aug '62), and the remnants consolidated with the Army of the Potomac with McClellan in overall command. Again he was at his best, reorganizing the weary and dispirited forces in the eastern theater. When Lee took his Army of Northern Virginia north of the Potomac McClellan (mistakenly believing he was outnumbered almost 2 to 1) cautiously advanced and intercepted the Confederates near Sharpsburg, Md.

At Antietam (17 Sep '62) he remained at his headquarters on the east bank of Antietam Creek and permitted the battle to be fought in detail by subordinates, who fought Lee's numerically inferior force to a draw. Lee's army was allowed to withdraw into Virginia and when McClellan could not be induced to pursue without reinforcements he was replaced by Ambrose Burnside (7 Nov '62) and sent home to await orders that never came.

In November '64 McCellan was the unsuccessful Democratic candidate for President and resigned his commission on election day. After the war he was chief engineer of the NYC Dept. of Docks (1870-1872) and Gov. of N.J (1878-1881). He always overestimated his opponent's strength and consistently demanded more men throughout operations. Lincoln once remarked that sending reinforcements to McClellan was like trying to "shovel flies across a barnyard."

BURNSIDE, Ambrose Everett.
1824-1881, Indiana
USMA 1847 (18/38); Arty.

After service in Mexican and Indian wars, Burnside resigned in 1853 to manufacture firearms in Bristol, R.I.; patented breech-loading carbine (1856); maj. gen. R.I. Militia (1855-'57); treasurer of Illinois Central R.R. in 1861. Entered Civil War as colonel of 1st Rhode Island Volunteers; commanded brigade at Battle of First Manassas (21 Jul '61) and promoted brig. gen.; led successful expedition against coastal installations in N.C. (Jan-Mar '62),

61

gaining promotion to maj. gen. and CG, IX Corps.

In August Burnside's IX Corps began moving from the Carolinas to join Maj. Gen. John Pope's Army of Virginia. While Burnside remained at Falmouth to forward arriving troops the IX Corps was temporarily commanded by Maj. Gen. Jesse Reno, where it participated in the battles of Second Manassas (29-30 Aug '62) and Chantilly (1 Sep '62). After these battles Pope's army was broken up and absorbed into the Army of the Potomac.

On 14 Sep '62 Maj. Gen. George McClellan, then commanding the Army of the Potomac, placed Burnside in command of the "Right Wing," (there does not appear to have been a "Left" or "Center" wing) comprising the IX and Maj. Gen. Joseph Hooker's I Corps. With Reno's death at South Mountain Brig. Gen. Jacob Cox temporarily assumed command of the IX Corps. The following day Hooker's I Corps was "temporarily detached" from the Right Wing. Burnside's wing, therefore, was reduced to one corps.

At Antietam (17 Sep '62) the IX Corps were placed on the left of the Union Army, where it eventually crossed Antietam Creek at the lower bridge to assault Lee's right flank. The timely arrival from Harpers Ferry of Confederates under Maj. Gen. A.P. Hill drove the IX Corps back to the bridge.

In November, when Lincoln grew weary of McClellan's failure to aggressively pursue Lee, Burnside was offered command of Army of Potomac. He accepted (Nov 7) only on the urging of other generals who did not want Hooker to have the position. After his defeat at Fredericksburg (13 Dec '62), Burnside was replaced by Hooker and sent to the Western Theater.

As commander of the Army of Ohio (25 Mar. - 12 Dec. '63) Burnside succeeded in the capture of Morgan's Raiders and the siege of Knoxville, Tennessee. Returning east in January 1864 to again assume command of the IX Corps, Burnside participated in Grant's overland campaign from Wilderness to Petersburg. After charges of mishandling troops in the Petersburg mine assault (30 Jul '64) he was relieved of command and resigned in April 1865 after a court of inquiry found him at fault in the attack.

After the war he was successful in engineering and managerial work with several railroads; Governor of Rhode Island in 1866 and twice re-elected; then served as U.S. Senator from that state until his death. A six foot, handsome man of impressive mien, he was described by Grant in his memoirs as "an officer who was generally liked and respected. He was not, however, fitted to command an army. No one knew this better than himself." Famous for his mutton-chop whiskers, his name is still associated with that barber's specialty.

FRANKLIN, William B.
1823-1903, Pennsylvania
USMA 1843 (1/39); Engrs.

Franklin served in the Mexican War (2 brevets) and until the Civil War was in Washington charged with construction of the new Capitol dome. On 14 May '61 he was appointed col., 12th U.S. Inf. (capt. since 1857), and brig. gen. three days later. At First Manassas (21 Jul '61) he commanded a brigade. In command of a division (3 Oct '61-18 May '62), he was then CG, VI Corps, Army of the Potomac (to 16 Nov), participating in the Peninsula Campaign (Mar-Jul '62, maj. gen., USV 4 Jul) and South Mountain at Crampton's Gap (14 Sep).

At Antietam (17 Sep '62) Franklin's VI Corps acted generally as a reserve near the North and East Woods, although some elements were engaged near the Dunker Church. After Fredericksburg (13 Dec '62), when Franklin commanded the "Left Grand Division" near Hamilton's Crossing, Burnside charged him with disobeying orders during the battle and relieved him of command. After months of "awaiting orders" Franklin was sent on the Red River Expedition as commander of the XIX Corps (20 Aug '63-2 May '64) where he was wounded at Sabine Crossroads.

While back east on sick leave for his wound his train was captured 11 Jul '64 by Early's men as they marched toward Washington, but he escaped the next day. He saw no further service in the field, serving on boards and again "awaiting orders" until the end of the war. He resigned from the R.A in 1866. From then until 1888 he was vice-president and general manager of Colt Firearms Manufacturing Company and held various minor public offices.

HOOKER, Joseph
1814-1879, Massachusetts
USMA 1837 (29/50); Arty.

During the Mexican War he won brevets in all grades through lieutenant colonel for gallant and meritorious conduct, a record not surpassed by any lieutenant in the service. He served as assistant adjutant general of the Pacific Division, 1848-49, was on leave of absence 1851-52, and resigned his commission 21 Feb '53 to take up farming. He soon regretted his decision and from 1858 attempted to regain a commission. It was not until 6 Aug '61, however, that he was commissioned brig. gen. of volunteers. The following spring, during the Peninsula Campaign, Hooker's division led the van of Heintzelman's III Corps. A press wire reading, "Fighting - Joe Hooker," appeared throughout the North as "Fighting Joe Hooker." Hooker never lived the sobriquet down.

In the ensuing actions of the Seven Days (25 Jun-1 Jul '62) and Second Manassas (29 Aug '62) Hooker exhibited solid qualifications as a combat officer in charge of his division and then of the I Corps. At South Mountain (14 Sep '62) the I Corps outflanked the Confederate defenders at Turner's Gap and at Antietam three days later Hooker's corps was chosen to spearhead the morning attack on Lee's left flank.

During Fredericksburg (13 Dec '62) Hooker's "Center Grand Division," consisting of the III and V Corps, acted as a reserve, although some elements participated in the action. After Burnside's defeat at Fredericksburg Hooker was placed in command of the Army of the Potomac (25 Jan '63).

In the Chancellorsville Campaign (Apr-May '63) Hooker maneuvered 135,000 troops across the Rappahannock and Rapidan Rivers with great adroitness, and outflanked Lee's Army of Northern Virginia. When it seemed Hooker was about to crush Lee's army of 60,000, he suddenly went on the defensive and dug in. In what has been called Lee's greatest battle Hooker was out generaled, outmaneuvered, and forced back across the rivers. When the Confederate army undertook the Gettysburg Campaign Hooker skillfully deployed his forces as to cover Washington and Baltimore which won him the thanks of Congress. However, when he was refused the reinforcement of the Harpers Ferry garrison Hooker asked to be relieved and was replaced by George Meade (28 Jun '63) three days before the Battle of Gettysburg.

In September he was sent west with the XI and XII Corps (Howard and Slocum), which were consolidated into the XX Corps. At Chattanooga in November '63, Hooker's troops chased Confederate skirmishers off Lookout Mountain in what became known in song and story as the "Battle of the Clouds." Grant, who was present and in overall command of Union forces, later stated "there was no such battle even worthy to be called a battle on Lookout Mountain."

At this time Hooker was a brig. gen. in the Regular Army and a maj. gen. of volunteers. After the death of James McPherson in front of Atlanta Sherman promoted Hooker's subordinate Howard to command the Army of the Tennessee and Hooker asked to be relieved from command in "an army in which rank and service are ignored." Thereafter he exercised departmental command until retiring in 1868 as a maj. gen.

Appraisals of Hooker's accomplishments, morals and military know-how have been the subject of discussion for more than a century. Known for his hard drinking and rough language, Hooker's headquarters were said to be frequented by a class of females known as "hookers," (a pre-Civil War term denoting women of questionable virtue), headquarters to which it was said "no gentleman cared to go and no lady could go."

MANSFIELD, Joseph
1803-1862, Connecticut
USMA 1822 (2/40); Engrs.

Served as Taylor's chief engineer during the Mexican War (3 brevets, 1 wound), later named col. and I.G. by Secretary of War Jefferson Davis (1853). At the beginning of the Civil War he was CG, Dept. of Washington (28 Apr '61-15 Mar '62), having been breveted brig. gen., R.A., (6 May '61) and promoted to that rank eight days later. Appointed maj. gen. (18 Jul '62), he was in a command under Gen. Wool at Fort Monroe, when, after months of politicking for a field command, he was assigned the XII Corps, Army of the Potomac (15 Sep '62). Although breveted for gallantry during the Mexican War Mansfield had never commanded soldiers in combat. At Antietam (17 Sep '62), worrying that his recruits (many were new levies) might break and run if not kept tightly bunched, Mansfield marched his corps to the front in a formation known as "column of companies, closed in mass." As he struggled to deploy his men from this unwieldy mass into a battle formation in the East Woods he was struck by a bullet and mortally wounded. Carried to a nearby house, he died the following day.

PORTER, Fitz-John.
1822-1901, New Hampshire
USMA 1845 (8/41); Arty.

Porter fought in the Mexican War (1 wound, 2 brevets) and served as a artillery and cavalry instructor at West Point and on the frontier. Appointed col., 15th U.S. Inf. 14 May '61 (bvt. capt. since 1856) and appointed brig. gen., USV three days later. Chief of Staff of the Dept. of Pa. and to Banks and Patterson in the Valley until October when he commanded a division in the Army of the Potomac (3 Oct '61-18 May '62), during which he directed the siege of Yorktown (5 Apr-4 May '62) in the Peninsula Campaign (brig. gen., USA 27 Jun '62). Appointed CG, V Corps, he was appointed maj. gen., USV on 4 Jul '62, leading his corps through the Seven Days (25 Jun-1 Jul '62) and Second Manassas (29-30 Aug '62). After the latter battle (the V Corps was then attached to Pope's Army of Virginia) Porter was relieved of command by Pope "for disobedience, disloyalty, and misconduct in the face of the enemy." Pending a court-martial Lincoln allowed Porter to retain command during the crisis of the Maryland Campaign. After Antietam (17 Sep '62), where the V Corps was held in reserve in the Union Center, Porter was relieved (5 Nov '62) and when a court-martial upheld Pope's charges Porter was cashiered from the Army (10 Jan '63). Porter later became a mine superintendent in Colorado, a merchant, and NYC commissioner of police, fire, and then public works. In 1869 he turned down an offer of a commission in the Egyptian Army. Porter spent the rest of his life in an effort to vindicate his name and have it reinstated on the Army roster. It was not until 1886, however, after a new hearing overturned his conviction, that he was reinstated, without back pay, as col. of inf., to rank from 14 May '61, and placed on the retired list.

SUMNER, Edwin V.
1797-1863, Massachusetts

Appointed directly to the R.A. in 1819, Sumner served in the Black Hawk and Mexican wars, the Kansas disturbances, and Indian fighting, earning the nick-name "Bullhead," after a musket-ball supposedly bounced off his head. He was appointed brig. gen., 16 Mar '61 and assigned CG, Dept. of the Pacific, 25 Apr-20 Oct '61. When corps organizations were established in the Army of the Potomac Sumner was given command of the II Corps (13 Mar-7 Oct '62) which he led in the Peninsula Campaign (Mar-Jul '62). During that campaign he was wounded twice and extolled by McClellan for "extreme gallantry." For service at the battle of Seven Pines (31 May '62) he was breveted maj. gen. R.A. and advanced to maj. gen. of volunteers on Jul 16. At Antietam (17 Sep '62) he led two divisions of his corps onto the field, riding at the head of the column instead of near the end to facilitate coordination. When his troops were attacked in the rear and flank Sumner attempted to rally his men but both divisions were thrown back to the North Woods, ending, for all practical purposes, the unit's role in the battle. At Fredericksburg (13 Dec '62) Sumner commanded the "Right Grand Division" of the army, consisting of his own and the IX Corps, unsuccessfully attacking the infamous stone wall at the foot of Marye's Heights. Upon the accession of Hooker to command the Army of the Potomac (26 Jan '63) Sumner asked to be relieved. Assigned to the Department of Missouri Sumner died enroute on 21 March.

SELECTED BIOGRAPHICAL SKETCHES
OF CONFEDERATE LEADERS IN THE MARYLAND CAMPAIGN

DAVIS, Jefferson
1808-1889, Kentucky
USMA 1828 (23/33); Inf.-Dragoons.

After West Point Davis spent the first seven years of his army career on the Northwest frontier. Eloping with Zachary Taylor's daughter, he resigned as 1lt. (1835) and settled down in Miss. as a planter, his wife dying three months after their marriage. In 1845 he remarried and was elected the same year to the US Congress, resigning the following year to fight in the Mexican War. While commanding a volunteer regiment known as the "Mississippi Rifles" he was severely wounded at Buena Vista.

Davis declined the appointment of brig. gen. USA in 1847 and instead was elected to the US Senate. In 1853 he was appointed Sec. of War by Pierce, served four years then re-entered the Senate, serving there until Jan '61, when Miss. seceded. Appointed maj. gen. of the State Militia, he was chosen provisional president of the government set up by the Confederate Congress at Montgomery, Ala., and inaugurated there on 9 Feb '61. In November he was elected to a six-year term of the permanent government at Richmond and inaugurated on Washington's Birthday in Feb '62.

As the war progressed, Davis kept a close hand upon the management of the Confederate armies. His war secretaries served as little more than clerks as Davis supervised the affairs of the department. To Lee alone does he appear to have conceded preeminence. He made frequent trips to the field, arriving at First Manassas as the fight was ending, and was under fire at Seven Pines. Later he toured the Western Theater. His handling of high command was extremely controversial. There were long standing feuds with Beauregard and Johnston, and his defense of generals such as Bragg and Pemberton irritated many in the South. On the political front his autocratic ways fostered a large and well organized anti-Davis faction in the Confederate Congress, especially in the senate. Issues arising from strong states rights sentiments did much to hamper Davis' efforts. When the President suspended habeas corpus, some states reacted by refusing to hold prisoners arrested under the act. The Georgia legislature even "nullified" Davis' act by declaring it unconstitutional. It was not uncommon for state governments to obstruct tax collection and to interfere with the process of conscription for constitutional reasons.

Newspapers proved to be a constant source of criticism of the government. The Richmond Examiner, The Charleston Mercury, and a number of other influential southern papers denounced the President regularly. Under these conditions Davis was never able to accumulate wartime powers in the Confederate Presidency such as Lincoln assumed in the North.

With the fall of Petersburg imminent Davis fled Richmond (2 Apr '65) with his cabinet for Danville, calling on his people to resist to the last and promising the recapture of the capitol. After Lee's surrender (9 Apr '65) the group turned south, where Davis was captured one month later at Irwinsville, GA. He was held for two years at Fort Monroe, accused of complicity in the Lincoln assassination. He was finally released (13 May '67) and after travel in Europe, and several unsuccessful business ventures, he settled in Biloxi, Miss. He died in poverty at the age of 82.

LEE, Robert E.
1807-1870, Virginia
USMA 1829 (2/46); Engrs.

Scion of a prominent Va. family, Lee served at Forts Pulaski, Monroe, and Hamilton, before being superintending engineer for St. Louis harbor. In 1846 he was sent to San Antonio as assistant engineer but soon joined General Winfield Scott in the Vera Cruz expedition. During the Mexican War (1 wound, 3 brevets) Lee's extraordinary industry and capacity won him the lasting confidence and esteem of Scott and he emerged from the war with a brilliant reputation. He then supervised the construction of Fort Carroll in Baltimore Harbor, until his appointment as superintendent at West Point (1852-55). Being in Washington when John Brown made his raid on Harpers Ferry (1859), Lee was sent to capture the raiders with a force of Marines from the Navy Yard. At the beginning of the Civil War, at Scott's urging, Lincoln offered Lee command of the Federal armies (18 Apr

'61). Lee declined, and resigned two days later to take command of Va. troops. After his first campaign in the field led to failure at Cheat Mountain, W. Va. (10-15 Sep '61) Lee commanded forces along the South Atlantic coast before being recalled to Richmond. Serving as military advisor to Davis until 1 June '62, Lee succeeded J. E. Johnston (wounded during the Peninsula Campaign) in the command of the force that then became known as the Army of Northern Virginia. Lee then embarked upon an offensive campaign known as the Seven Days Battles in which the Federal Army of the Potomac fell back from Richmond. With the immediate danger to the Confederate capitol ended Lee moved against a second Federal army, the Army of Virginia under John Pope. After defeating Pope at Second Manassas (29-30 Aug '62) Lee was determined to retain the initiative and crossed the Potomac into Maryland in his first invasion of the North. McClellan, having been placed in command of the combined troops of his own and Pope's forces, moved to counter the Confederate maneuver. When McClellan came into possession of Lee's march orders Lee was forced to concentrate his army along Antietam Creek near Sharpsburg, Md. In the Battle of Antietam (17 Sep '62) the two armies fought to a bloody stalemate and Lee recrossed the Potomac two days later.

After McClellan was replaced by Ambrose Burnside the new Federal commander attempted to move on Richmond by way of Fredericksburg. In the Battle of Fredericksburg (13 Dec '62) Lee successfully blocked the maneuver and both armies went into winter quarters.

In the spring, after achieving his military masterpiece at Chancellorsville (1-4 May '63), Lee's army was too weakened by the death of Jackson and dwindling supplies of manpower and material ever to recover its former combat effectiveness. Furthermore, the Federal armies were increasing in strength and proficiency and competent military leadership was finally being found. The high tide of the Confederacy was reached when Lee was unable to destroy the Army of the Potomac at Gettysburg (1-3 Jul '63) and was forced to retreat into Va. Coming East from the simultaneous and equally decisive victory at Vicksburg, Grant assumed command of all Federal armies, formulated an over-all strategic plan, and then proceeded to destroy Lee's Army of Northern Virginia in a costly 11-month campaign of attribution. It was not until Feb. of 1865 - two months before the surrender - that Lee was given over-all command of all Confederate armies. Accepting the presidency of Washington College, after the war, he served until his death (22 Oct '70) at the age of 64, and was buried there. (The name was later changed to Washington and Lee University).

HILL, Ambrose Powell
1825-1865, Virginia
USMA 1847 (15/38); Arty.

Hill served in the Mexican War, the Seminole wars and on the frontier before resigning 1 Mar '61 as 1st Lt. Commissioned col. 13th Va., he served in W. Va. and was in the reserve at First Manassas (21 Jul '61). Stationed in northern Virginia during the winter of 1861-62, he was appointed brig. gen. (26 Feb '62) and placed in command of a brigade. He fought in Williamsburg, Virginia before being promoted maj. gen. (26 May) and leading his division at Mechanicsville, Gaines Mill and Frayser's Farm. Called "Hill's Light Division" for its speed in marching, this unit was sent to Jackson's corps after Hill quarreled with Longstreet, where it fought at Cedar Mountain (9 Aug '62) and Second Manassas (29-30 Aug '62).

In the Antietam Campaign Hill's division was one of several under Jackson assigned to capture Harpers Ferry. After the surrender of that post (15 Sep '62) Jackson's forces rejoined Lee at Sharpsburg, while Hill's division remained to parole Federal prisoners. On 17 September Hill's division marched 15 miles to rejoin Lee. In the afternoon, as Burnside's IX Corps was threatening to turn Lee's right flank, Hill arrived and drove the Federals to the banks of Antietam Creek.

At Fredericksburg (13 Dec '62) Hill's command occupied Hamilton's Crossing, south of the town, and helped repel the Union attacks of Meade and Gibbon.

Hill marched with Jackson during Chancellorsville (1-4 May '63) and succeeded him until wounded himself. Named lt. gen. (23 May '63), Hill took command of the newly-created III Corps, leading it through the battles of Gettysburg (1-3 Jul '63) and Wilderness (5-6 May 64), during both of which he was ill. As a corps commander he did not live up to expectations. Douglas Freeman wrote of Hill: "He does not fail beyond excuse or explanation; he does not succeed....It may be because of ill health or a sense of larger, overburdening responsibility." Hill performed somewhat unevenly and was often incapacitated. He was on sick leave during the period 8-21 May '64, during which Ewell assumed temporary command of the III Corps. Hill rejoined his corps for North Anna, Cold Harbor, and the Petersburg campaign. In the

71

latter he rose to his greatest heights as a corps commander. In late Mar '65 he was again away on sick leave. On 2 April, while returning to his unit at Petersburg he was shot and killed by a Union straggler. Freeman wrote that although Hill was "genial, approachable, and affectionate in private life, he was restless and impetuous in action." His wife was the sister of John Hunt Morgan.

**JACKSON, Thomas Jonathan
("Stonewall")
1824-1863, Virginia
USMA 1846 (17/59); Arty.**

Having received the brevets of captain and major during the Mexican War, Jackson resigned his commission (1852) to become an instructor at Virginia Military Institute. At the beginning of the Civil War Jackson became a colonel of Virginia militia and was ordered to command at Harpers Ferry. In May he was superseded by Joseph Johnson and promoted to brig. gen. the following month. After distinguished service at First Manassas (21 Jul '61) - where he and his brigade earned the sobriquet "Stonewall" - Jackson was promoted to maj. gen. (7 Aug '61). In November he was dispatched to the Valley, where he waged the magnificent Valley Campaign the following year against three Federal armies (May-Jun '62). After defeating his adversaries, and forcing the Government at Washington to withhold reinforcements from McClellan's army threatening Richmond, Jackson joined Lee's forces in the Seven Days Battles (25 Jun-1 Jul '62). Jackson's lightning-like turning movement against Pope in August was a crucial factor in the victory that followed at Second Manassas (29-30 Aug '62).

In the Maryland campaign Jackson captured the Federal garrison at Harpers Ferry before rejoining Lee at Sharpsburg in the Battle of Antietam (17 Sep '62).

In October Lee reorganized the Army of Northern Virginia and Jackson was promoted lieut. gen. and made commander of the Second Corps. He commanded the right wing in the victory at Fredericksburg (13 Dec '62). His career reached its high point in the famous flank march around Hooker's right at Chancellorsville (1-4 May '63). Later that same night (2

May) Jackson was accidently shot by his own men. He died on 10 May of pneumonia, which developed after amputation of his left arm.

LONGSTREET, James (Pete)
1821-1904, South Carolina
USMA 1842 (54/56); Inf

Longstreet served in the Seminole wars, the Mexican War (1 wound, 2 brevets), and on the frontier before resigning 1 June '61. Appointed brig. gen., 17 June '61. At First Manassas (21 Jul '61) he commanded a brigade. Promoted maj. gen. 7 Oct. '61, he commanded a division at Yorktown and Williamsburg and led the right wing at Fair Oaks and Seven Pines. In the reorganization that followed the Peninsular campaign he was given command of a wing containing over half of Lee's infantry. During Second Manassas (29-30 Aug '62) his command fell on the Union left flank to route the Federals. His command fought well at Antietam and he was promoted lt. gen. 9 Oct '62. Shortly thereafter his command was reorganized and designated the First Corps, Army of Northern Virginia. At Fredericksburg (13 Dec '62) his command again performed with distinction. In February '63 Longstreet was sent to the Suffolk, Va. as commander of the Confederate Department of North Carolina and Southern Virginia.

Rejoining Lee's army after Chancellorsville (1-4 May '63), Longstreet joined the army's march into Pennsylvania. He was opposed to the Gettysburg campaign in general and instead favored an offensive by Lee in the West. But since Lee was determined to invade Pennsylvania, Longstreet felt the campaign should be strategically offensive but tactically defensive and had the erroneous impression that Lee subscribed to this theory. His delay in attacking on the second day at Gettysburg, and his perceived lethargy in organizing "Pickett's Charge" on the third exposed him to the most vindictive criticism by Southerners after the war. Douglas Freeman points out, however, that "Lee never gave any intimation that he considered Longstreet's failure at Gettysburg more than the error of a good soldier."

In Sept '63 Longstreet was sent with two of his divisions to support Bragg in the West. After the Battle of Chickamauga he was sent to oppose Burnside in the Knoxville campaign. In 1864 Longstreet led his command back to join Lee for the Wilderness campaign. There, he was seriously wounded (6 May '64) by his own men, almost precisely a year after Jackson had been mortally wounded under similar circumstances nearby. Longstreet was out of action until 19 Oct, when he returned to command the forces at Bermuda Hundred and those north of the James River. He participated in the Petersburg campaign in the spring of '65 and joined Lee's army on the march to Appomattox Court House, and surrender.

After the war Longstreet became president of an insurance company, served as U. S. Railroad Commissioner, and Minister to Turkey.

STUART, James Ewell Brown
("Jeb")
1833-1864, Virginia
USMA 1854 (13/46);
Mounted Rifles-Cav.

Stuart served on the frontier in Indian fighting (seriously wounded) and in Kansas during the border disturbances. While on a leave of absence he was Lee's volunteer A.D.C. during John Brown's raid on Harpers Ferry (1859). Resigned 3 May '61 as Capt., he determined to follow his state, although his Va.-born and West Point educated father-in-law, Philip St. George Cooke, stayed with the Union. Stuart was commissioned lt. col. of the Va. Inf. on 10 May '61 and 14 days later was named capt. of C.S.A. Cav. During that summer he was at Harpers Ferry and First Manassas. Appointed brig. gen., C.S.A. 24 Sept '61. At the beginning of the Peninsular campaign he commanded cavalry at Williamsburg and in June '62 led his troops in his "ride around McClellan." He then fought in the Seven Days' Battles and at Harrison's Landing and as maj. gen. (25 July '62) took command of all the cavalry in the Army of Northern Virginia. He fought at Second Manassas (29-30 Aug '62), and at Antietam (17 Sep '62) his horse artillery held Lee's left flank near the Potomac River. He led his cavalry division in the Second Corps at Fredericksburg and succeeded A. P. Hill temporarily

74

as commander of Jackson's Corps (3 May 63) at Chancellorsville. In the Gettysburg campaign Stuart's Cavalry Corps fought the battle of Brandy Station (9 Jun '63) and a number of famous cavalry skirmishes before undertaking the fateful Gettysburg raid. His cavalry fought on the third day at Gettysburg and was held in check by Gregg's cavalry. Stuart fought in the Wilderness and Spotsylvania campaigns and was mortally wounded (11 May '64) at Yellow Tavern. He died the next day. Satirically called "Beauty" by his West Point classmates, the five-foot nine Stuart wore a massive and flowing beard, purportedly to cover a receding chin and certainly to camouflage his youth. His personal bravery, endurance, panache, and high good humor made him a magnificent cavalry leader. Stuart's staff was excellent, and he trained his subordinates with a sober professionalism. Deeply religious and not unlike his good friend Jackson in his sincerity and piety, he also had a wide streak of vanity and exhibitionism in his make-up that contrasted strangely with the other qualities.

9 781782 663867